BATHROOM BOOK
of
WASHINGTON TRIVIA

Weird, Wacky and Wild

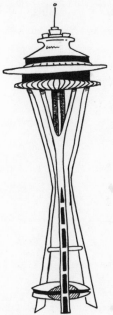

Gina Spadoni & Lisa Wojna
Illustrations by Roger Garcia

BLUE
BIKE
BOOKS

© 2007 by Blue Bike Books
First printed in 2006 10 9 8 7 6 5 4 3 2 1
Printed in Canada

The Publisher: Blue Bike Books

Library and Archives Canada Cataloguing in Publication

Spadoni, Gina, 1970–
    Bathroom book of Washington trivia : weird, wacky and wild /
Gina Spadoni and Lisa Wojna.

ISBN-13: 978-1-897278-18-5
ISBN-10: 1-897278-18-7

    1. Washington (State)—Miscellanea. I. Wojna, Lisa, 1962– II. Title.

F891.5.S62 2007   979.7   C2006-906406-7

ISBN 10: 1-897278-18-7
ISBN 13: 978-1-897278-18-5

Project Director: Nicholle Carrière
Project Editor: Nicholle Carrière
Illustrations: Roger Garcia
Cover Image: Roger Garcia

We acknowledge the support of the Alberta Foundation for the Arts for our publishing program.

PC: P5

ACKNOWLEDGMENTS

I would like to thank a few people who helped me in putting
this book together: Faye Boer of Folklore Press and my publisher
and editor Nicholle, for providing me with the chance and helping me through the process; my parents, especially my dad Don,
whose own life spent in Washington lent me endless bits of
trivia to include; my lovely sisters Renee and Andrea, who
I could always count on for a late-night chat and laugh; the
Capitol Hill Library, which happily lent me all of its books on
Washington; my dear friends, who let me blather on about the
factoids I've been learning; and finally, many thanks to my
"fabulous fellow," Matt, whose constant support and humor
just can't be beat and without whom I wouldn't have nearly as
much fun.

–*Gina Spadoni*

Many thanks to: my clever editor Nicholle, who pieced together
the work of two authors and did so seamlessly; to my mentor
Faye, who always gives more of herself than required; and to my
family—my husband Garry, sons Peter, Matthew and Nathan,
daughter Melissa and granddaughter Jada. Without you, all this
and anything else I do in my life would be meaningless.

–*Lisa Wojna*

CONTENTS

INTRODUCTION

Having been born and raised in Seattle and calling it home for most of my 36 years, the opportunity to write this trivia book was very exciting. I lived in Boston, Massachusetts, while obtaining my master's degree, and when I was flying home for the first time after many months away, I found myself breaking into tears as I took in the gorgeous landscape covered in water and the striking green, rolling hills from the plane window. My intense reaction surprised both me and my seatmate, but it also taught me something important: I really loved this place and wanted to live in it—as my choice rather than because it was where I was born.

Washington is a state full of amazing history, topography and people, and exploring it is something I never tire of doing, either in person by traveling around or vicariously by learning about various people and things in books or in movies or on television. I hope I manage to impart some of the wonder of the state to those that read this book, and—if it is a place you live now—that you find something new to explore, cherish and share with others.

WHAT SETS WASHINGTON APART

Washington's diversity—in its geography, its weather, its people—sets it apart from the rest of the nation.

Research measuring the "creative vitality" of the state has shown it to be well above national benchmark averages, likely the result of strong support for art, reading, music and theater. The Seattle International Film Festival, for example, is the most-attended and longest-running film festival in the nation. Washington residents go to creative events, hang out in coffee shops, listen to music and buy it, too, in numbers that surpass almost all other states. Even Washingtonians' use of public libraries is significantly higher per capita than the vast majority of other states.

Why is all of this the case? What's really going on here? Some speculate that it's the weather; maybe—goes the theory—the overcast skies lead to more introspective, artsy-type activities. Others think it's just the type of person attracted to the laid-back Washington culture. That somehow, a devotion to denim draws more intellectual, bookish types. As the techie population continues to grow more quickly than the state's number of musicians and writers, it will be interesting to watch for any cultural change. That said, a Washingtonian techie might actually be qualitatively different than a techie from California or Boston...

The Seattle–King County nonprofit sector is supported more strongly than any other in the country, as measured by the income per capita of the nonprofit arts sector—$133.34 compared to the national average of $51.85. So, not only do those in the area attend more events and thus drive up collected nonprofit art sector revenues, but they also give more money in charitable donations than the national average.

IN THE BEGINNING

Why Washington?

Originally, the area now occupied by the Pacific Northwest
state of Washington was originally called the Territory of
Columbia—a fitting tribute to the powerful Columbia River.
But when the territory became a state, the name was changed to
Washington. It's most commonly believed the name change was
to honor George Washington, the first American president. But
some sources suggest the change may have been made to avoid
confusion with the District of Columbia.

A Newbie Comes on Board

Washington was the 42nd state to be admitted to the Union
on November 11, 1889. It is the only state to have been named
after a president, and residents there proudly refer to themselves
as "Washingtonians."

DID YOU KNOW?

Washington boasts three nicknames: the Evergreen State, the
Green Tree State and the Chinook State.

Size versus Status

Washington's largest city is Seattle, with a population of
563,374. However, the much smaller city of Olympia, which is
actually the state capital, doesn't even rate as one of the state's
top 10 cities when it comes to population. It only boasts just
over 44,000 residents according to the 2000 census.

SYMBOLS AND EMBLEMS

The Great Seal

The first emblem officially adopted by the State of Washington was the Great Seal in 1889. Honoring the state's namesake, a bust of President George Washington is the central feature.

DID YOU  **KNOW?**

While it's not certain when the Chinook phrase *Al-ki* or *Alki*, meaning "by and by" or "hope for the future," was adopted as Washington's official motto, the term made its first appearance on a territorial seal designed by Lieutenant J.K. Duncan of Governor Steven's surveying expedition, dated 1853.

Official Flag

It wasn't until Washington had been a state for 34 years that it adopted its official flag in 1923. Again, President George Washington is prominently featured as the Great Seal is centered on a dark green background.

The Complexities of Floral Arrangements

There's nothing like the vibrant reds, pinks and purples of the rhododendron to announce the advent of spring. And for the residents of Washington back in 1892, it was this welcome beacon of spring they chose to name as their state's official flower. The initial push to choose a floral symbol of the state was in preparation for the World's Fair to be held in Chicago the following year. The reasoning behind this was so that Washington women would have an official flower to enter in a floral exhibit. To that end, ballot boxes were set up across the state in an effort to get the opinions of as many women as possible. The choice was narrowed to a battle between clover and the rhododendron, and the "rhodie" emerged victorious with 53 percent of the 15,000 votes—enough for the Washington Senate to approve it as the official state flower on February 10, 1893.

It turns out the declaration was a tad premature, since only half of the Washington Legislature agreed to the decision. And it was a debate that continued for 66 years, until on February 10, 1949, both the Washington Senate and the Washington Legislature passed a law agreeing to the naming. In 1959, Leonard Frisbie added his own spice to the pot by lobbying for an amendment to the 1949 law, adding that the specific variety of rhododendron to represent Washington should be *Rhododendron macrophyllum* or coast rhododendron.

Other Symbols and Emblems

☞ The western hemlock was named the state tree in 1947.

☞ In 1951, the willow goldfinch became the state's official bird.

☞ Anglers applauded the announcement of the steelhead trout as the state fish in 1969.

☞ You might have to see a sample of this to believe it, but in 1975, petrified wood became the state's official gemstone.

☞ Swing that partner 'round and 'round! In 1979, the square dance became Washington's official dance.

☞ Bluebunch wheatgrass was adopted as the state's official grass in 1989.

☞ Also in 1989, the apple was designated as the state fruit.

☞ The Asett tartan—a green cloth with blue, white, yellow, red and black stripes—is the state's official tartan. It was designed in 1988 and adopted in 1991.

☞ Even insects managed a little recognition among Washington folk, when in 1997, the green darner dragonfly was named the state's official insect.

☞ The next year, in 1998, the Columbian mammoth was named the state's official fossil.

☞ And in 2005, the orca was named Washington's official marine mammal.

DID YOU KNOW?

Washington has both an official song and an official folk song. In 1959, "Washington My Home," written by Helen Davis and set to music by Stuart Churchill, was designated as the official state song. And in 1987, Woody Guthrie's "Roll On Columbia, Roll On," was adopted as the state's official folk song.

DID YOU  KNOW?

As befits a port state, Washington has an official state ship. The 860-foot-long container ship named the *President Washington* was given that honor in 1983. Boasting a 43,000-horsepower diesel engine, the *President Washington* is considered one of the largest container ships ever built in the U.S.

City Symbols and Other Neat Stuff

☛ The great blue heron was named Seattle's city bird on March 13, 2003. The city's flower is the dahlia, named on November 19, 1913, its song is "Seattle the Peerless City," named on May 1909, and its motto became the "City of Flowers" on October 7, 1942.

☛ Tacoma has been known as the "City of Destiny" for more than 100 years.

☛ Spokane is known as the "Lilac City."

☛ Yakima is known as the "Palm Springs of Washington," according to a privately erected sign on Interstate 82. On a more official note, in the 1950s, the city fathers of the day marketed the city as the "Fruit Bowl of the Nation." The city of just over 229,000 residents boasts four sister cities overseas: Morelia, Mexico; Itayangi, Japan; Derbent, Russia; and Keelung, Taiwan.

☛ Bellingham also enjoys relationships with four sister cities: Port Stephens, Australia; Punta Arenas, Chile; Tateyama, Japan; and Nakhodka, Russia.

AVERAGES AND EXTREMES

Coast or Mountains?

Tucked away in the northwest corner of the country, Washington borders the province of British Columbia, Canada, to the north, the Pacific Ocean to the west, and the states of Oregon to the south and Idaho to the east. The influences from the ocean, coupled with a varied topography that includes the mountains of the Cascade Range and Mount Olympus, directly influence the varied climate that the state typically experiences in any given season.

As a result, mean temperatures and precipitation rates can be quite extreme from one part of the state to another. For example, communities along the coast can expect 85 inches or more of rain each year, as in the case of Aberdeen, while more mountainous areas might expect only 12 inches. Yakima, for example, often only receives 8 inches of rain in a calendar year.

Temperature variations are also common. While folks nearer the Pacific could be enjoying balmy spring and early summer weather, it could be well into July before some mountain passes are cleared of snow and safe for hiking.

Average Annual Precipitation
Roughly speaking, when it comes to precipitation, Washington is almost equally divided into east and west regions. The west, bordering the Pacific Ocean, can expect anywhere between 30 and 100 inches each year, with some areas as high as 140 to more than 180 inches. The majority of the eastern region typically receives less than 30 inches of precipitation.

Highest Temperatures

Ice Harbor Dam recorded Washington's highest temperature on August 5, 1961. It was a steaming hot 118°F on that day.

Lowest Temperatures

Washington's all-time low was recorded at Mazama and Winthrop on December 30, 1968—a frigid –48°F.

Average Scores

☞ Richland earns first place when it comes to recording the warmest average annual temperature, at 54.1°F.

☞ Kennewick, on the other hand, records the warmest average month in the state. Typically, the weather in July averages 90.4°F.

☞ If you prefer cooler weather, Mazama earns the prize for the coldest average annual temperature of 43.9°F.

☞ The winner of the coldest average month, however, goes to Winthrop. January in that community averages a chilly 10.9°F.

☞ The community with the wettest annual average measurements goes to Forks, with 121.7 inches of precipitation expected each year.

☞ Aberdeen, on the other hand, wins out when it comes to having the month with the wettest average precipitation. That community can expect an average of 21.9 inches of precipitation during the month of December.

☞ The areas that can expect the driest weather are Desert Aire and Priest Rapids Dam, with an average annual precipitation of only 6.84 inches.

The Most Snow in a Day

The winner for the largest snowfall in a 24-hour period goes to Winthrop. A total of 52 inches of the white stuff fell on January 21, 1935.

Snow, Snow...

According to data collected by the National Climatic Data Centre, U.S. Department of Commerce, between the years of 1948 and 2006, the highest daily snowfall recorded at the Seattle-Tacoma International Airport occurred on January 13, 1950. A total of 20 inches fell that day.

Records collected between 1898 and 2005 from Cedar Lake also indicated a high of 20 inches falling on December 28, 1898, and again on January 27, 1923.

...and More Snow

Weather data for Bellingham International Airport from 1949 to 1996 point to far less snow falling in that location. The all-time high was on December 4, 1980, with little more than 9 inches of snow falling that day.

Record Rainfalls

☞ In 1998, an accumulation of 11.73 inches of rain descended on Washington's Sea-Tac Airport—a record breaker for the month of November.

☞ Mount Mitchell takes top honors for the most rainfall in a 24-hour period. A total of 14.26 inches fell over the midnight hours, from November 23 to 24 in 1986.

☞ Centralia gets the prize when it comes to the most rainy days in a row. From November 1996 to February 1997, it rained continuously for 55 days.

THE WORST WEATHER

The Top 10

Washington is no stranger to extreme weather events. In fact, the National Weather Service calls the state one of the "nation's leaders in presidentially declared weather-related disasters." Here are the extremes that made it onto the top 10 list:

10. In November 1990, there was such extreme statewide flooding, especially on the rivers in the northwest, that the floating bridge on Lake Washington on Interstate 90 sank. Total damage was estimated at $250 million, and two deaths were blamed on the event.

9. Seattle is known for many things, including its "greatest snowstorm," which the city endured in late January and early February of 1916. Seattle recorded its largest snowfall in a 24-hour period during that storm, with 21.5 inches on February 1, contributing to a total accumulation that month of 35 inches. Other parts of the state reported receiving anywhere between two and four feet of snow during the storm.

8. The flooding of major rivers in the west and southeast of the state contributed to an estimated $800 million in damage in February 1996. Three Washingtonians lost their lives in that flood, which was the highest on record for many southwest Washington rivers. Flooding spread to neighboring Oregon and north Idaho.

7. On April 5, 1972, a series of tornadoes whipped through the cities of Vancouver and Spokane, giving the state the dubious honor of leading the nation in tornado deaths that year. Six people perished that day, and another 300 were injured. An estimated $50 million in damage was reported.

6. The Stevens Pass Avalanche of March 1, 1910, is considered the deadliest avalanche in U.S. history. Ninety-six people died when the two passenger trains they were riding in were swept into a ravine by the avalanche's powerful force.

5. The northeast face of Mount St. Helens was destroyed by a volcanic eruption on May 18, 1980, killing 60 people, flooding the Columbia River with mud and ash and turning the skies black. Residue traveled for thousands of miles, affecting neighboring states and Canadian provinces alike.

4. Three million acres of forest were lost between August 20 and September 9, 1910, because of forest fires in east Washington and north Idaho. The fire was said to have created its own weather. Eighty-five people, 72 of them firefighters, died in the blaze.

3. The second largest dump of snow experienced by Washingtonians occurred on January 13, 1950. On that date, a blizzard hit the Puget Sound area, leaving behind 21.4 inches of snow in a 24-hour period. The blizzard claimed 13 lives, and with the average temperature a chilly 34.4°F, the winter of 1949–50 has the distinction of being Seattle's coldest winter on record.

2. Everyone loves the promise of a warm spring. But in May and June of 1948, warm temperatures resulted in the greatest spring snowmelt flooding on record. Rivers overflowed like never before. And on May 30, in the span of just an hour, the flooding in Washington contributed to the complete destruction of America's largest wartime housing project, the city of Vanport. It was Oregon's second largest city at the time, with a population of 35,000, and was located on the floodplain of the Columbia River. The flood lasted a record-breaking 45 days.

1. Finally, Washington's number one weather event of the 20th century is said to be the Columbus Day windstorm. On October 12, 1962, wind gusts in Bellingham and Vancouver were measured at up to 150 miles per hour, and gale-force winds of similar strength occurred in several parts of the state. It was considered the strongest non-hurricane windstorm to strike the continental U.S. in the 20th century, claiming 46 lives, destroying 15 billion board feet of timber and tallying up an amazing $235 million in property damage.

Other Extreme Conditions

☛ The state experienced a tornado outbreak, so to speak, on May 31, 1997. Six tornadoes touched down on Washington soil that day—an astounding number when you consider the record number of tornado touchdowns for an entire year, prior to that date, was four in 1989. That same day, some locations reported severe thunderstorms with flash floods and gusting winds, as well as hail as large as 3 inches in diameter. By the end of 1997, Washington had recorded 14 tornados.

- On January 20, 1993, an immense windstorm on the state's west coast claimed five lives and cost $130 million in damage.

- The years 1976 and 1977 were the driest in Pacific Northwest history. Drought conditions produced poor crop yields, and most areas instituted some form of water rationing or restrictions on power consumption.

- To say it was a heat wave is an understatement. In August 1967, Spokane reported 11 consecutive days with temperatures 90°F and warmer.

GENERAL GEOGRAPHY

The Big Picture

Depending on the source, Washington can be divided into as many as six recognized geophysical regions. They include:

- ☛ the Olympic Mountains;

- ☛ the Coast Range (which includes the Willapa Hills and Portland Basin);

- ☛ the Puget Sound Lowlands;

- ☛ the Cascade Mountains;

- ☛ the Columbia Plateau (which includes the Columbia Basin and Blue Mountains);

- ☛ and the Rocky Mountains.

These regions are further grouped into what are considered three major geographic zones: the Interior, the Cascades and the West and the Pacific Coast.

Size Matters

Washington is considered the 18th largest state in the U.S., boasting an area totaling 71,342 square miles. Rectangular in shape, generally speaking, Washington measures 360 miles from west to east and 240 miles from north to south.

Front and Centre

Chelan County, just 10 miles west-southwest of Wenatchee, is considered the state's geographic center. Occupying more than 2900 square miles, Chelan Country is a mountainous region. Its highest peak is Bonanza Peak at 9511 feet above sea level and its deepest known point, in Lake Chelan, is 400 feet below sea level.

Highest Point

Mount Rainier boasts the highest elevation in the state, measuring 14,410 feet at its highest point.

Middle of the Road

When all the numbers are in, the mean elevation in the state is 1700 feet.

Lowest Point

Washington's lowest elevation can be found in the depths of the Centralia Coal Mine. The deepest pit is 820.21 feet below sea level.

Glacier Ice

Washington boasts more glaciers than all the other 47 contiguous states combined.

- ☛ Mount Rainier has 25 major glaciers that cover nearly 34 square miles.

- ☛ There are 318 glaciers in North Cascades National Park. Glaciers in the park and surrounding areas cover about 42 square miles.

- ☛ Glaciers cover about 18 square miles of the Olympic Mountains.

All Points West

The tip of the Olympic Peninsula is the most northwesterly point in the U.S.

DID YOU KNOW?

One hundred million years ago, an island now known as the Okanogan Terrane collided with North America. Prior to this geographic event, Washington as we know it was situated under the Pacific Ocean. Another similar collision between two large bodies of land 50 million years ago resulted in the creation of the Cascade Range.

Momentous Moments in Geography

A tsunami thought to be caused by a gigantic earthquake on January 26, 1700, is said to be the first recorded weather event in the Pacific Northwest.

One Big Family

Thirty-nine counties make up Washington State:

Adams	Grays Harbor	Pierce
Asotin	Island	San Juan
Benton	Jefferson	Skagit
Chelan	King	Skamania
Clallam	Kitsap	Snohomish
Clark	Kittitas	Spokane
Columbia	Klickitat	Stevens
Cowlitz	Lewis	Thurston
Douglas	Lincoln	Wahkiakum
Ferry	Mason	Walla Walla
Franklin	Okanogan	Whatcom
Garfield	Pacific	Whitman
Grant	Pend Oreille	Yakima

Location, Location, Location.

The city of Seattle was founded in 1851. The area's new settlers were keen to establish a significant trading port like that on America's eastern seaboard, so they originally named the area "New York Alki." One of the city's founders, David Swinson ("Doc") Maynard was the loudest voice calling for the new city to be named after Chief Sealth (Seattle in English). And while Seattle may not be the New York of the West, because it's situated on a narrow strip of land between Puget Sound and Lake Washington, the city's main economy has everything to do with the shipping industry.

DID YOU  KNOW?

The town of Seattle was actually incorporated twice, the first time in 1865. It was unincorporated on January 28, 1867, because of a petition circulated by several of the town's citizens, then it was incorporated again in 1869.

Humble Beginnings
What started as a neighborhood sawmill turned into Spokane, Washington's second largest city. Officially founded in 1871, Spokane also became a centre for railway traffic.

Claim to Fame
Tacoma was settled in 1852 by an assortment of immigrant families. Most notably, a Swede named Nicholas De Lin built the first "water-driven mill" in the area.

SUPER-NATURAL PARKS

National Parks

Protecting the natural beauty of Washington has always been a priority. Following the example of Yellowstone National Park, Wyoming, which made international history as the world's first national park in 1872, Americans became more conscious of the need to protect the natural beauty around them.

Washingtonians were quick to jump on that bandwagon, establishing one of the first four national parks in the U.S. with Mount Rainier National Park in 1899. Today, Washington boasts three national parks:

☛ Mount Rainier with 378 square miles (235,612.5 acres) of parkland;

☛ North Cascades with 788.72 square miles (504,781 acres) of parkland;

☛ Olympic National Park, which is the largest, occupying an area of 1400 square miles (896,000 acres). Ninety-five percent of this has been designated "formal wilderness." Since its inception, it has been named a UNESCO Biosphere Reserve and World Heritage Site.

State Park System

The United States held its first National Conference of State Parks in 1921. By that time, setting aside natural spaces for conservation and recreational enjoyment had become an accepted practice. Washington was among those states setting the standard for others, having already established seven state parks, while 29 other states had yet to establish their first! Today, Washington boasts a total of 120 state parks.

One of a Kind

The Hoh Rain Forest, located in Olympic National Park, is the only rainforest in the U.S., giving the park international status as a Biosphere Reserve and World Heritage Site. Accumulating upwards of 150 inches of rainfall each year, trees and other vegetation grow at a phenomenal pace. The park is home to Washington's largest tree, the "Rain Forest Monarch." The giant Sitka spruce is 668 inches (55.67 feet) in circumference, 191 feet tall and has a 96-foot crown (or wingspan, were it a bird). Estimates place the tree's age at between 500 and 550 years old.

PEAK EXPERIENCES

Naming Mount Rainier

British explorer Captain George Vancouver was the first to record seeing Mount Rainier in 1792. While the area's indigenous peoples called the volcanic mountain Tah-ho-ma, Vancouver named it Mount Rainier after his dear friend, Rear Admiral Peter Rainier. Rainier, a member of England's Royal Navy, served with the British East India Company, made his way through the ranks to Admiral of the Blue, served during the American Revolutionary War and was even elected a member of the British Parliament.

DID YOU KNOW?

The first white settlers to successfully reach the summit of Mount Rainier did so on August 10, 1870. Led by a Yakima guide, Hazard Stevens and Philemon Van Trump made the 10-plus hour hike—and they left a brass plaque at the summit to prove it!

Mountain Ranges

There are 15 distinct mountainous areas or ranges in Washington:

Black Hills	Olympic Mountains
Blue Mountains	Pacific Coast Ranges
Cascade Range	Selkirk Mountains
Chiwaukum Mountains	Sourdough Mountains
Columbia Mountains	Stuart Range
Issaquah Alps	Wenatchee Mountains
Manastach Ridge	Willapa Hills
Monashee Mountains	

Wenatchee Treasure

The Wenatchee Mountains checker-mallow, a rare plant on the endangered species list, is only found in the Wenatchee Mountains along Peshastin Creek, south of Leavenworth.

Willapa Hills Heights

The highest point in the Willapa Hills is Boistfort Peak, measuring 3061 feet above sea level. The Willapa Hills are considered the lowest uplands in the entire Pacific Coast Range system.

The Black Hills are located in Capitol State Forest and are part of the Willapa Hills.

Pacific Coast Mountains

The Pacific Coast Range spans much of North America's west coast. Its contributions to Washington State include the Olympic Mountains and the Cascade Range.

The Cascade Range's claim to fame is its connection with the "Ring of Fire," a "ring" of volcanoes located around the Pacific Ocean. The Cascade volcanoes are responsible for all the volcanic eruptions in the continental United States. In the last 100 years or so, there were a series of eruptions on Lassen Peak in 1914 to 1921 and Mount St. Helens erupted in 1980. More recently, minor eruptions of Mount St. Helens were been reported in 2005.

The Olympic Mountains may not be the highest peaks in Washington, but their western slopes, which face the Pacific Ocean, are considered the wettest place in the 48 contiguous states. The Hoh Rain Forest, which is located there, has recorded as much as 142 inches of rainfall.

As Old as the Hills
According to geologists, the Selkirk Mountains are older than the Rocky Mountains. They were named after Thomas Douglas, Fifth Earl of Selkirk.

Sourdough Sights
The Sourdough Mountains are located north of Mount Rainier National Park, but a hike on one of the range's trails provides a clear view of the famous peak.

Volcanic Roots
While the Stuart Range, located in central Washington, doesn't have an active volcano, it's believed the range was created from the batholithic—volcanic or "fire rock" located beneath the earth's surface—roots of former volcanoes in the Cascades more than 100 million years ago.

Crossing Borders

While the majority of the Monashee Mountains (78 percent) are located in British Columbia, Canada, the remaining 22 percent stretch south 329.33 miles and east-west 93.21 miles, attaching themselves to the Columbia Range.

The Columbia Mountains also span a considerable portion of British Columbia—75 percent. The remainder of the range runs through Montana, Idaho and Washington.

The Blue Mountains are primarily located in Oregon, but meander through the southeast portion of Washington.

Issaquah Alps

The Issaquah Alps are located, not surprisingly, near Issaquah. A portion of Washington's I-90, from Lake Washington to the Cascade Mountains, travels along the base of this range.

Central Washington Peaks

The Mantash Ridge is part of the Cascade Range located in central Washington in Kittias and Yakima Counties. It's home to the Manastash Ridge Observatory, a research station maintained by the astronomy department of the University of Washington.

Also located in central Washington are the Chiwaukum Mountains. These mountains are made of schist, a metamorphic rock made up of a combination of minerals, quartz and feldspar.

WATER

As Far as the Eye Can See and Then Some

Washington State has upwards of 3000 miles of shoreline, of which 157 miles is coastline, so it's little wonder that Washingtonians love oceanside activities. To protect these areas for conservation and recreation, the "powers that be" established Deception Pass State Park, the state's first marine park complete with "marine facilities" in 1922. Today, there are 40 marine parks in the state, with more than 7600 feet of public moorage space to enjoy.

A Water-lover's Paradise

Washington boasts about 1000 lakes. Of these, long and narrow Lake Chelan is the largest, measuring 55 miles in length with a width between one and three miles at any given spot.

Water, Water Everywhere

About six percent (4721 square miles) of Washington is covered by water. Major rivers include the Columbia River, Snake River and Yakima River. Lake Franklin D. Roosevelt and Lake Washington are considered the state's major lakes.

DID YOU  KNOW?

Most of the lakes in King County were formed as far back as 16,000 years ago by glacial ice receding across the area.

Must-see Marine Wonders

Are you looking for a seaside picnic with an added punch? Why not stop by Lime Kiln Point State Park? Located on the west side of San Juan Island, the site is well known as a prime location for whale watching.

Kind Donations

Another must-see for water lovers is Moran State Park. Located on Orcas Island on about 5200 acres of land that boasts both saltwater and freshwater shorelines, the park was acquired in small parcels between 1920 and 1991. Much of this was through donations from the Moran family.

ENVIRONMENTAL ISSUES

Garbage In, Garbage Out

While Washington's industries continue producing too much pollution, real progress is being made. In 2003, Washington ranked 38th of all the states and provinces in North America for releases and transfers—a considerable reduction from previous years (in fact, a 47 percent decrease from 1998, when it ranked 34th).

Ecosystem in the Balance

Many Pacific salmon species are threatened or endangered according to the criteria of the Endangered Species Act. While many factors have led to this unfortunate reality, the main reasons are habitat destruction or modification, which includes such things as hydropower dams, agricultural practices, urbanization and forest practices. In an effort to revitalize the ecosystem and return it to health, the EPA joined other federal and state agencies, counties, tribes and forest landowners and re-evaluated its regulations. The result is that the forest practices in Washington are now among the most stringent in the nation.

DID YOU KNOW?

Washington is unique in that so much of its power comes from water, via hydroelectric power plants. In 2003, a whopping 73 percent of all power generated in the state was hydroelectric. Much of it was produced by the Grand Coulee Dam, which supplies approximately 20 billion kilowatt hours of electricity per year!

While Washington therefore has the lowest power-related air emissions in the nation, protecting and preserving native fish species such as the salmon is challenged by hydroelectric dams.

Radical E-Waste Program

March 2006 marked Washington's passage of one of the most extensive electronic waste recycling laws in America, providing a free system paid for by the manufacturers of electronic equipment, with retailers and others volunteering to act as collection points. The program is meant to reduce the amounts of lead, mercury and other dangerous chemicals from discarded electronic products currently being dumped in Washington landfills and being exported to developing countries.

NATIVE ANIMALS

Wildlife Still Wild

As a large part of the land in Washington is still forested, many animals still thrive in the wild. Black bears, elk and deer are plentiful, as are mountain goats at certain elevations. Mountain lions still exist in the mountain ranges of the Cascades and Olympics, and coyotes, bobcats, beavers, foxes, otters and raccoons are native throughout the majority of the state. Many of these animals still live in greenbelts in developed communities and are spotted at trash receptacles or merely crossing the street in neighborhoods on both sides of the state. Coyotes and raccoons sometimes pose challenges to local cats and dogs.

For the Birds

The bald eagle, a regal bird if ever there was one, is native to Washington. It has been challenged in years past by habitat disruptions but has been growing in population as conservation efforts have increased.

Sandhill cranes, listed as endangered in Washington since 1981, are also often spotted at the Columbia National Wildlife Refuge in Othello.

Mama Mia Mammals!

The enormous and majestic orca makes its home in the waters of Puget Sound for much of the year, and pods swim throughout the Strait of Juan de Fuca. While sightseeing trips specifically for whale watching are common, a simple ferry ride through the San Juans often yields the surprise of a leaping whale. Gray whales are also indigenous but tend to spend their time in deeper waters.

ENDANGERED SPECIES

Spotlight on the Wolf

Gray wolves, also known as timber wolves, were once at home in the Cascade mountain ranges. Fur trappers helped destroy their populations, but the final blow came in the early 1900s, when the government took action against them because of the complaints of farmers and ranchers, who resented the wolves' hunting capabilities (livestock was easy prey for them). The gray wolf has been an endangered species in the state for many years, but in the 1990s, biologists began spotting packs in the mountains. It is believed that they may be migrating back to Washington from Canada.

At Risk

Forty animal species were listed as threatened or endangered in Washington in 2006, including the Columbian white-tailed deer, woodland caribou, brown pelican, pygmy rabbit, gray wolf, bald eagle, Aleutian Canada goose, peregrine falcon, brown pelican, northern spotted-owl, grizzly bear, marbled murrelet, Oregon silverspot butterfly, snowy plover, humpback whale, sea otter and three species (green, loggerhead and leatherback) of sea turtles. The state also has 43 endangered plant species, including the golden paintbrush, Nelson's checker-mallow, Sabine's lupine, Pacific pea, rosy owl-clover and northwest raspberry.

Saving the Salmon

Perhaps the most famous part-time "residents" of Washington aren't people, but salmon. There are seven indigenous salmon and trout species in Washington and Oregon (chinook, coho, chum, sockeye and pink salmon, and steelhead and cutthroat trout), with their habitat extending from tiny inland streams out to the Pacific Ocean.

Sadly, because of past commercial fisheries, habitat loss, hatchery problems and a changing ocean environment, salmon numbers have been declining for many decades. Since a 1992 study, 214 salmon stocks in the Pacific Northwest have been considered to be threatened or endangered under the Federal Endangered Species Act, and 17 spawning salmon stock are considered to be extinct. This is, of course, disconcerting.

Not only are salmon a long-standing part of the culture in the Northwest, but they are also an important part of the ecosystem. Losing them would lead to other losses, some that we know about and others that may not become known until it is too late. Species that depend on the salmon as a key part of their ecosystem include bears, eagles, mink and river otters.

When the salmon population declines, so do these populations; they are inextricably linked. Unfortunately, too, the dams on the Snake and Columbia Rivers also impact the salmon, though it isn't known to what extent.

DID YOU  KNOW?

Steelhead and rainbow trout are actually the same species—it's just that rainbow are from fresh water and steelhead from salt water. And steelhead and cutthroat trout are now classified in the salmon genus, *Oncorhynchus*, having recently been moved from the trout genus, *Salmo*.

Burrowing Pocket Gophers

Mazama or western pocket gophers primarily live underground. Their bodies have evolved to make them especially good burrowers—their lips can be closed behind their front teeth, and their particularly soft and loose pelts let them go both backwards and forwards through their tunnels easily. In Washington, several populations of pocket gophers have evolved into separate subspecies, some of which are now extinct—those remaining are rare. The Mazama pocket gopher is a state endangered species candidate and has been proposed as a federal candidate as well.

 During the Klondike Gold Rush period in Seattle in the late 1890s, dog thieves became prevalent. Unsavory salesmen would sell any sort of dog for pulling sleds through Alaska. Families locked up their pets. One woman, Beulah Gronlund, decided to take action—she helped form the first Seattle Humane Society and got laws passed forbidding such cruelties.

DANGEROUS CREATURES

Rattlers

Washington lucked out in the reptile category—the only poisonous snake living within its borders is the western rattlesnake, which generally relegates itself to the eastern side of the state, since the weather is better suited to it there. This snake has a large, triangular head that is significantly wider than its neck, a diamond-shaped pattern along the middle of its back and rattles on the tip of its tail. It comes in a plethora of colors ranging from olive to brown to gray. Full-grown snakes range from 18 inches long all the way up to about 4 feet.

DID YOU KNOW?

Contrary to what you might see in cartoons, rattlesnakes actually don't like people and won't bite unless they feel threatened. Luckily, rattlesnake bites rarely contain enough venom to kill a human, but bites can be painful, swell and cause skin discoloration.

DID YOU KNOW?

Garter snakes, rubber boas and western rattlesnakes deliver live offspring from eggs held in their bodies until hatching. All other Washington snakes lay eggs in safe areas that have enough warmth for hatching.

Aggressive House Spider

Otherwise known as *Tegenaria agrestis*, the hobo spider is the most poisonous of the spiders that a Washingtonian is likely to see. They are brown, about one to two inches long and have relatively hairless, smooth bodies. They run fast and tend to gravitate towards garages and basements. These spiders are said to be aggressive because they will actively go in for a bite if cornered. While the bite hasn't proven venomous enough to do serious (or deadly) damage, it will sting, become red, spread out two to six inches, blister, become raw and oozy—and take weeks or possibly months to heal. It is important to seek medical attention if bitten. These spiders are found particularly in Seattle and Pullman, especially in the fall.

DID YOU KNOW?

All spiders are poisonous, but most are too small or contain venom that is too weak to affect humans significantly.

BOTANICAL BONANZA

Natural Vegetation

Washington boasts more than 1300 species of plants. Trees native to the state and prevalent in western forested lands include the Douglas-fir, Sitka spruce, western red-cedar and western hemlock. Washington also has hardwood tree species, including the bigleaf maple, vine maple, red alder, madrone, black cottonwood and Oregon ash.

As eastern Washington has a different, much drier climate, the trees that thrive there differ. Characteristic species include the ponderosa pine, western white pine and western larch, along with greasewood and sagebrush.

Small trees and shrubs indigenous to the state include the dogwood tree, Pacific yew, salal, moss, mountain phlox, fern and the huckleberry, which has fruit similar to the blueberry but more tart. Many long-time Washingtonians have a special fondness for the huckleberry, as it brings back memories of childhood hikes and special pies made from the pickings.

Wildflowers in the state are numerous—in fact, over 3000 species grow in Washington. They include pink fireweed, brown-eyed Susan, monkeyflower, Flett's violet, goldenrod, Oregon grape, piper bluebell, sunflower, red Indian paintbrush, purple lupines, yellow poppies, deerhead orchids, wakerobins and the western rhododendron (the state flower). The rhododendron blooms in a near rainbow of colors, including white, red, yellow, pink and orange, and its leaves stay green and glossy year round.

Fields of Grain

Washington is the largest producer in the nation of soft white wheat, growing enough to yield $815 million in revenue. Two different types of soft white wheat are grown in the state, club and common. Club wheats have shorter, more compact heads than common types. A combination of the two types make up one of the world's most popular wheat mixes, called western white, which is only available from the Pacific Northwest.

Wheat is the state's third largest farm product, after apples and milk, and Washington ranks fifth in the nation of largest wheat growers by volume. What's fascinating is that wheat farmers in Washington have a leg up on all other wheat farmers, as each wheat-acre produces significantly more wheat product than other states. This is attributed to climate, soils and progressive growers. Up to 90 percent of the wheat grown in Washington goes overseas to countries such as Japan and Pakistan.

DID YOU KNOW?

Interestingly, soft white wheat is an essential ingredient in most confectionery products. Thank goodness for Washington!

Number One Fruit Production

In 2004, Washington was the number one producer in the U.S. of red raspberries (90 percent of total U.S. production), hops (75 percent), apples (58 percent), sweet cherries (47.3 percent), pears (42.6 percent), Concord grapes (39.3 percent) and Niagara grapes (31.6 percent).

IMPORTS AND INVADERS

The Dandelion

Not indigenous to the state, the common dandelion was brought here and planted by Doc Maynard's second wife, Catherine. Dandelion tea was often used as a tonic back in the early 20th century.

British Weed Crosses the Pond

Spartina anglica, otherwise known as English cordgrass, unfortunately arrived in Puget Sound in 1961 and is now a class B noxious weed. The Washington State Department of Agriculture (WSDA) formed the Noxious Weed Control Board in 1997 and has been working to reduce the amount of English cordgrass and other noxious weeds since then. So far, they've managed to remove about 10 percent of *S. anglica*.

Murderous Grass

Cheatgrass was brought from Eurasia to Washington in the 1890s and spread rapidly through the state, particularly its most arid areas in the eastern region. Cheatgrass grew rampantly, and within 30 years was found not only in Washington, but also in Nevada, Utah, Idaho and parts of many other states, too! It grows thickly and effectively shuts out sunlight needed by microbiotic crusts—a layer of earth at or just below the ground's surface that is important to ecological health. Basically, cheatgrass uses all the nitrogen that other plants would normally take up. In addition, the nitrogen increases the cheatgrass' susceptibility to fire, a real problem in arid, desert-like areas.

The Hermaphrodite Bivalve

The Pacific oyster was brought to Washington from Japan in 1922. Oddly, the oysters start life as males and then after a year, start functioning as females. While the Pacific oyster is considered to be one of the state's most valuable shellfish, its introduction to the area unfortunately resulted in the accidental move here of several other invasive species, including the Japanese littleneck or Manila clam, the Japanese oyster drill and brown algae. Key Pacific oyster spawning beds are located in Puget Sound, Hood Canal, Grays Harbor, Tillamook Bay, Coos Bay and Morro Bay.

NATURAL DISASTERS

Avalanche Buries
Great Northern Railcars at Wellington

In March 1910, one of the worst train catastrophes in U.S. history occurred near Stevens Pass in the Cascade mountain range, taking a total of 96 lives. The cause was said to be a combination of rain, lightning, locomotive sparks and clear-cutting. The avalanche claimed the highest number of victims the state had ever seen in a natural disaster, including 35 passengers, 58 railroad employees sleeping on the two trains involved in the avalanche and three railroad employees sleeping in cabins.

The Dry Falls and Scablands

The Dry Falls are just that—bone dry. They are the dramatic remains of what was once the largest waterfall on earth (at least that we are aware of!). They encompass 3.5 miles of 400-foot-high cliffs. In contrast, Niagara Falls is a mere one mile wide with only a 65-foot "fall."

So how did this enormous fissure come to pass? During an event called the Missoula Flood, 3000 square miles of water broke free of an ice dam and ran clear through the Idaho panhandle, the Spokane River Valley, quite a bit of eastern Washington and then on to Oregon...culminating in the flood of Portland, which it buried under 400 feet of water. The topographical changes wrought by this amazing force left the Dry Falls. The scablands that surround the area are lesser versions of similar erosion "events" and were caused by other, less violent ice age floods. Time frame? Somewhere between 10,000 and 15,000 years ago.

The 1994 Forest Fires
The Leavenworth-Chelan area sustained devastating fires in the summer of 1994, signs of which are still visible. The great blaze destroyed 170,000 acres in just two weeks—the result of summer storms that hit the area with thousands of lightning strikes.

DID YOU  KNOW?

Leavenworth's 1994 fires raged from July 24 to December 24, during which time 2400 firefighters from a total of 24 different states worked side by side trying to save the city. Part of what made fighting the blaze so difficult was that the fire was moving so fast—it was traveling at over 50 miles per hour!

DID YOU KNOW?

The 1980 eruption of Mount St. Helens was more powerful than 300 Hiroshima-sized nuclear bombs. Clouds of ash rose 12 miles into the sky, and ash was deposited as far away as Maine.

Blowing Its Top

May 18, 1980, began like any other day, but realization quickly dawned that this would be a Sunday morning like none other in recent Washington history. At 8:32 that morning, Mount St. Helens erupted as the result of an earthquake measuring 5.1 on the Richter scale. Here's what happened:

☛ The eruption lasted nine hours;

☛ Almost 230 square miles of forest were destroyed;

- The explosion blew a crater 1968.5 feet deep and almost one and a half miles wide from rim to rim on the mountain's face;

- It was estimated the speed of the subsequent landslide was between 70 and 150 miles per hour;

- As much as 600 feet of debris were deposited in the nearby North Fork Toutle River;

- An estimated 7000 big game animals were killed in the blast;

- An estimated 12 million chinook and coho fingerlings and another 40,000 young salmon were destroyed;

- Sixty people living near the mountain were killed.

In 1982, the president and Congress established the 110,000-acre Mount St. Helens National Volcanic Monument as a site for research, recreation and education.

DID YOU  KNOW?

While climbing enthusiasts have scaled Mount St. Helens' rocky face for years, the volcano itself wasn't reopened for climbing until July 2006. Mountaineers can now go as far as the crater rim, but entry into the crater is still prohibited.

EARLY INHABITANTS

First Footers

Some scholars credit Sir Francis Drake, as well as Chinese and Polynesian explorers, as being the first to explore the Washington coastline as early as 1579. A Spanish expedition led by Juan de Fuca, a Greek navigator, was credited with traveling the Northwest Passage.

But among the first explorers to set foot on Washington soil were Spaniards aboard the *Santiago* and *Sonora*, two ships led by Captain Don Bruno de Heceta in 1775. This first contact led to the Spanish claiming the area all the way to Russian territory in the far north (now Alaska) for Spain.

The famed Captain James Cook and a group of British explorers first sighted Cape Flattery three years later, but a British contingent didn't explore the area until 1789. Either way, explorers from both countries, as well as those from other nations, combed the area, scanning, mapping and getting to know the numerous tribes of Native Americans living there. And then, in 1819, Spain ceded its original claims to the territory to the U.S., beginning 27 years of disputed joint occupancy by Britain and the U.S. The issue was finally resolved when the Brits signed the Treaty of Oregon on June 15, 1846, and the land now known as Washington State became solely United States territory.

Original Occupants

Before explorers first set foot on what's now known as Washington State soil, the area was far from uninhabited. Indigenous peoples had established communities, complete with several permanent buildings of substantial size, at several sites along the Duwamish River. In fact, in 1933, a federal court stated that "in the mid-1850s, when the Indian treaties were signed, the 17 Duwamish villages had a total of more than 93 buildings…[and] the Duwamish tribe occupied land around Elliott Bay, the Duwamish River, Lake Washington and Lake Sammamish."

DID YOU  **KNOW?**

In the 1770s, an outbreak of smallpox and other diseases introduced to the area by European settlers decimated the Native American population in the Pacific Northwest.

Native Nations

There are 29 federally recognized Native American tribes or nations in Washington:

Chehalis	Muckleshoot	Skokomish
Colville	Nisqually	Snoqualmie
Cowlitz	Nooksack	Spokane
Hoh	Port Gamble S'Klallam	Squaxin Island
Jamestown S'Klallam	Puyallup	Stillaguamish
Kalispel	Quileute	Suquamish
Lower Elwha Klallam	Quinault	Swinomish
Lummi	Samish	Tulalip
Makah	Sauk-Sulattle	Upper Skagit
	Shoalwater Bay	Yakama

☞ Each tribe has a home reservation or trust land.

☞ Reservations or trust lands are found in 21 Washington counties and occupy 3.24 million acres of land.

☞ The largest reservation is the Yakama, which occupies 2,137.6 square miles.

☞ Yakima boasts a population of 31,799, of which only 7411 are American Indian or Alaska Native heritage and 10,605 are white.

☞ The smallest reservations include Jamestown S'Klallam, Stillaguamish and Sauk-Suiattle, occupying just a few acres of land each.

☞ Jamestown S'Klallam, perhaps one of the smallest reservations population-wise, boasts a total of 16 residents, of which 13 are white, two are American Indian or Alaska Native and one is multiracial.

☞ According to the 2000 census, there were 93,301 persons claiming only American Indian and Alaska Native heritage in the state.

DID YOU  KNOW?

An 1850 census numbered the population of Washington at 1201 persons. This figure likely did not include the state's indigenous population.

Family Histories

If you're into genealogy and your family name is Collins, Asselt, Denny, Low, Boren, Bell or Terry, you might find a settler among the members of your family tree. A number of settlers bearing these family names were among those who first homesteaded on Washington soil back in 1851 and 1852.

Japanese Washingtonians

As early as the 1880s, a large settlement of Japanese immigrants had established themselves in the Seattle area. These immigrants were harshly treated during World War II, when they were segregated in internment camps, a sad blemish on U.S. history.

This wasn't the first time an entire race was segregated. On November 3, 1885, all people of Chinese descent in Tacoma were herded out of the town like they were a plague of locusts. Jacob Robert Weisbach, the mayor at the time, called the Chinese "a curse and a filthy horde." About 350 individuals lost their homes and all their possessions. And it wasn't until more than 100 years later, in 1993, that the Tacoma city council officially apologized for the misguided notions of their earlier leaders.

BY THE NUMBERS

Population at a Glance

According to the 2000 census:

- ☞ 6.7 percent of Washinton's population was under five years old;

- ☞ 25.7 percent were under 18;

- ☞ 11.2 percent were 65 years and older;

- ☞ 50.2 percent were female;

- ☞ 10.4 percent claimed to be of foreign birth;

- ☞ 14.0 percent spoke a language other than English at home;

- ☞ 87.1 percent of the population aged 25 and older were high school graduates;

- ☞ 27.7 percent of the population aged 25 and older had earned a bachelor's degree or higher;

- ☞ 981,007 persons aged five and over suffered from a disability;

- ☞ the average home cost $168,300.

Major Cities

Based on population, the state's three major cities are Seattle, Spokane and Tacoma. Seattle is the largest, with a population of 573,911, followed by Spokane at 196,818 and Tacoma at 195,898. Vancouver and Bellevue aren't too far behind in the population count, with 157,493 and 117, 437 respectively. Interestingly enough, the state capital, Olympia, is much smaller, with a population of only 44,114.

Ethnic Breakdown

While Native Americans were Washington's first inhabitants, according to the 2000 census, they now only represent 1.6 percent of the state's population. Seventy-seven percent of Washingtonians are Caucasian, 8 percent are Hispanic, 6.3 percent are Asian, 4 percent are of two racial backgrounds and 3 percent are black.

Population by Race (2005 estimates)

Race	Population
White	5,115,347
African American	190,484
Native American	103,125
Asian	410,372
Hispanic	438,415

DID YOU KNOW?

In 1997, Washington ranked ninth when it came to its percentage population of Native Americans. At that time, 1.8 percent of Washington's population was of that ethnic background.

The Power of a Name

While it isn't clear what actually precipitates this trend, a review of the state's birth statistics make it quite clear what names folks prefer for their newborns. Statistics from the Washington Centre of State Health list the names Jacob and Ethan as the top two picks by new parents of boys in 2002, 2003 and 2004. In 2004, 515 Jacobs and 510 Ethans were born. For parents of girls, the names Emma and Emily were the top two picks over the same period, with 486 Emmas and 461 Emilys.

Population by State
(July 2005 estimates)

Ranking	State	Population
1	California	36,132,147
2	Texas	22,859,968
3	New York	19,227,088
4	Florida	17,789,864
5	Illinois	12,763,371
6	Pennsylvania	12,429,616
7	Ohio	11,464,042
8	Michigan	10,120,860
9	Georgia	9,072,576
10	New Jersey	8,717,925
11	North Carolina	8,683,242
12	Virginia	7,567,465
13	Massachusetts	6,398,743
14	**Washington**	**6,287,759**
15	Indiana	6,271,973
20	Wisconsin	5,536,201
25	South Carolina	4,255,083
30	Iowa	2,966,334
35	Nevada	2,414,807
40	Maine	1,321,505
45	Delaware	843,524
50	Washington, DC	563,523

DID YOU  KNOW?

Washington has the fifth largest Asian population in the U.S. at 6.3 percent. Persons of Chinese and Filipino ancestry make up the largest portion of that ethnic group.

Population per Square Mile
(2000 estimates)

State	Population
Washington, DC	9378
New Jersey	1134.5
Rhode Island	1003.2
Massachusetts	809.8
Washington	**88.6**
Wyoming	5.1
Alaska	1.1

DID YOU  KNOW?

According to the Office of Financial Management, from April 2005 to April 2006, the population of Washington increased by approximately 120,000.

Washington Population Through the Years

Year	Population	Density per square mile
1880	75,116	1.13
1890	357,232	5.37
1900	518,103	7.79
1910	1,141,990	17.16
1920	1,356,621	20.39
1930	1,563,396	23.49
1940	1,736,191	26.09
1950	2,378,963	35.75
1960	2,853,214	42.88
1970	3,413,250	51.29
1980	4,132,353	62.10
1990	4,866,669	73.13
2000	5,894,143	88.57

DID YOU KNOW?

The median age of Washingtonians is 36.24 years. But if you separate the men from the ladies, the average age of men is 35.25 years and the average age for women is 37.26. The difference lies in the fact that members of the fairer sex tend to live longer than their male counterparts. In 2004, of the 99,166 Washingtonians aged 85 and older, 31,804 were men and 67,362 were women.

Till Death Do Us Part?

In 2004, 40,169 couples tied the knot. Sadly, another 25,930 marriages ended in divorce that year.

Religious Convictions

Washingtonians consider themselves a devout group, with 68 percent of the population declaring themselves Christians. Forty-five percent of that Christian population is Protestant, 22 percent are Roman Catholic and the remaining one percent is listed as "other Christian." Only 2 percent of the population are members of another religion, and 27 percent admit to being non-religious.

ROADSIDE ATTRACTIONS AND TOURIST TEMPTATIONS

Tea Anyone?

You may not have heard of Zillah, but chances are if you were traveling on I-82 southeast of Yakima before 2003 and were in need of gas, you'll likely remember the spot. That's because what was once considered the oldest operating gas station in the country was likely the exact place where you needed to fill up. Gracing the station is a 15-foot-high teapot created in 1922 by Jack Ainsworth as a "political statement memorializing the Harding Teapot Dome scandal." The scandal, which began in 1921 under President Harding's tenure, revolved around the ownership of three oil fields, one located near Teapot Dome, Wyoming. The area got its name because of a large, teapot-shaped rock overlooking the area.

Although the gas station is no longer in service, the teapot is still there.

Spirits of Iron

Folks riding through the Ashford area might want to take a bathroom break at a sculpture park called Ex-Nihilo. That's where artist Dan Klennert has a permanent exhibit for what he calls his "Recycled Spirits of Iron." Among the many sculptures on display are an assortment of animals, birds, sealife, dinosaurs, people and even bikes and trains. The park is located on Route 706, just before the west entrance to Mount Rainier National Park.

DID YOU KNOW?

In Latin, *ex-nihilo*, means "something created from nothing." To make his iron sculptures, artist Dan Klennert acquires iron pieces and lets their shapes direct the kind of sculpture he creates.

Indigenous Artwork

Indian Painted Rocks is a small, 2000-square-foot state park outside Yakima that boasts an assortment of pictographs estimated to be 1000 years old. The pictographs are etched and painted on the face of a cliff along what was once a popular Native trail.

Carnation Goodness

Talk about the queen of milk production. Apparently, back in the 1920s, Segis Pietertje Prospect—a high-producing milk cow that each year pumped out 16,500 quarts of milk and enough cream to make 1400 pounds of butter—had the world of dairy farmers in awe. And so she should, since her output was as much as 10 times that of an average dairy cow of the day. So in order to give the grande dame the homage she so rightly deserved, the Carnation Research Farm erected the "World's Champion Milk Cow" statue. To sneak a peak at the monster monument, take a trip down Carnation Farm Road in Carnation.

Unique Art

A drive along North Pearl Street in Ellensburg will likely lead you past Dick and Jane's Art Spot. Actually a private residence, the yard is filled with a collection of wooden sculptures and is uniquely adorned with an assortment of items. A fence that sports a collection of thousands of reflectors along with portions of painted mural art surrounds the house. Buttons, lights, bottles, more than 10,000 bottle caps and a collection of recycled and found objects all add to the unique quality of this ever-changing family home. While resident artists Richard C. Elliott and Jane Orleman create much of the artwork, they are also art collectors and have the work of more than 40 other artists on display. The couple has been working on their home for 27 years—a wonderful way to live your calling.

For the Record Books

Talk about high-school memorabilia. The 18-foot-tall "Codger Pole of Colfax," which is surrounded by five cedar columns, each 22 to 36 inches in diameter, commemorates a much-disputed 1938 football game between Colfax and St. John high schools and the rematch that took place 50 years later. The faces of the 51 individuals who took part in the games were carved into the columns by chainsaw artist Jonathan LeBenne of Idyllwild, California. It is the largest chainsaw sculpture of human like-nesses in the world.

Miniature Churches

If you're into visiting unique churches, here are a couple you won't want to pass up. While miniature churches aren't an uncommon phenomenon, each has its own unique qualities. Washington boasts two miniature churches, one in Elbe and the other in Sultan.

The Elbe structure is known as the "Little White Church." It measures 18 feet by 24 feet, seats 46 people and was built in 1906 by German settlers. *Ripley's Believe It or Not* once heralded it as the "smallest church in America."

Sultan's church, on the other hand, is considerably smaller, measuring only 7 feet by 9 feet. It only takes eight people to bring this small place of worship to full capacity, but since its function is as its name implies, the Wayside Chapel is just the perfect size.

BIG THINGS

Big Foot Roams

Big Foot, aka Sasquatch or Yeti, is reputed to live somewhere in the woods in Washington and (much like the Loch Ness monster) has reportedly been seen many times, though there is no concrete evidence of its existence. That said, "Squatch" has long been the mascot of the Seattle Supersonics NBA basketball team (which, when this goes to press, may no longer be true, because the Sonics team was recently sold).

Larger Than Niagara Falls

Celilo Falls was one of the largest waterfalls by volume in North America—significantly dwarfing even Niagara Falls. Located on the Washington-Oregon border on the Columbia River, it provided Native Americans with ample fishing and was a heavily populated area for many thousands of years—estimates suggest between 10,000 and 12,000. In fact, Lewis and Clark noted that it was the most populated place they had come across on their journey west in 1805. Why isn't this a major honeymoon destination? Because the falls were destroyed during the building of the Dalles Dam, which effectively "drowned" the site on March 10, 1957. Ah, well, that's progress for you.

Walking (or Driving) on Water

The floating bridge connecting Seattle and Medina, known as the Governor Albert D. Rosellini–Evergreen Point Bridge, is the longest floating bridge in the world. Spanning 7578 feet (1.4 miles), construction of the bridge took a full three years, and the structure first opened to traffic on August 28, 1963. Thirty-three pontoons keep the bridge floating, and 62 anchors keep it from drifting away. There is a drawbridge in the middle that allows ships to pass, though it is not opened during major traffic hours. The bridge connects Seattle and Medina (home of Bill Gates) across Lake Washington.

Originally named the Evergreen Point Bridge, the structure was renamed in Governor Rosellini's honor in 1988 in recognition of his efforts to push ahead with the project despite the fact that the country was experiencing a recession. Should anyone desire to check, it's probably also a likely contender for the bridge with the longest name!

MUST-SEE PLACES

The Museum of Flight

A trip to a local landfill was likely never so providential—or so prosperous—as it was one day in 1965 when the remnants of a 1929 Boeing 80A-1 were discovered in Anchorage, Alaska. It was an amazing find, but one that required safe and careful recovery and many years of restoration. And so in 1965, the Pacific Northwest Aviation Historical Foundation, and the subsequent Museum of Flight, was born.

OPENING DAY

The museum first opened its doors in 1968, and remained in the 10,000-square-foot rented facility in Seattle Center until 1975, when it moved into the William E. Boeing Red Barn. Abandoned in 1909, the building was owned by the Port of Seattle, which planned to demolish it. Instead, the Museum of Flight took it off their hands for the grand sum of one dollar. A few years later, the building was designated an historic site, recognized as the oldest aircraft manufacturing plant in the United States, as well as one of the largest remaining all-wooden factory buildings west of the Mississippi River. By this point, a restoration project was underway on the old building. It re-opened in 1983.

RENOVATIONS

Since then, the museum has undergone a number of transformations and additions. Today, the museum's relatively small, 10,000-square-foot beginnings have expanded to an area of about 273,000 square feet.

MAIN ATTRACTIONS

Visitors can view the 1929 Boeing 80A-1, the flying machine that started it all and the only one of its kind, in the museum's Great Gallery. One other unique item is an aircraft on loan from the U.S. Air Force—the first "Air Force One," a Boeing VC-137B first delivered to President Dwight D. Eisenhower in 1959.

DID YOU KNOW?

The Museum of Flight boasts a collection of more than 150 historically significant air- and spacecraft and welcomes more than 400,000 visitors each year.

A Museum of Wonder

The Washington State History Museum, located in Tacoma, lays claim to some pretty unique items.

☛ A shingle-weaving machine is the largest artifact at the museum. When in operation, the machine was used to cut thin wedges from cedar logs.

☛ The oldest artifacts at the museum are 11,000 years old and may have seen the last ice age. Known as Clovis points, the spear-shaped implements, likely used in the same way we'd use a small knife today, are made from stone or bone.

☛ The most unique exhibit is likely the "Product Tree," a display of the history of the wood industry from 1880 to 1920 in three-dimensional form. Wheelbarrows, fence pickets and even caskets give visitors a picture of how important wood was to early settlers.

☛ As if frozen in time and providing an almost ghostly feeling, 35 mannequins depicting people from the state's past are on display in the Hall of Washington.

DID YOU **KNOW?**

And in case you were wondering, a sum total of 350,000 bricks were used to cover the entire museum.

Washington Park Arboretum

Established in 1934, the Washington Park Arboretum is located in Seattle's city center and consists of more than 200 acres of trees and shrubs hardy in the maritime Pacific Northwest. Considered a "living plant museum," the arboretum serves three main purposes: to show the natural beauty of each species collected; to demonstrate the state's natural ecology and diversity; and to conserve important species, including cultivated varieties, for the future.

THE EARLY DAYS

Originally, the park was founded by an agreement between the city of Seattle, the University of Washington and subsequently the Arboretum Foundation. But the union of the three groups hasn't been without its difficulties. Add to that concerns from the surrounding neighborhood and a few disagreements that have had to be settled over the years.

Still, the efforts of all involved in the project have resulted in the construction of historical features such as the Stone Cottage, gardens such as the Winter Garden and Woodland Garden, the development of the Center for Urban Horticulture and the creation of a master plan that strategically tackles issues such as what direction the educational and interpretation programs will take in the future.

Today, visitors to Seattle can enjoy the esthetic value of this natural gem in the middle of the city, while landscape enthusiasts and elementary school and university students alike can learn from this natural wonder.

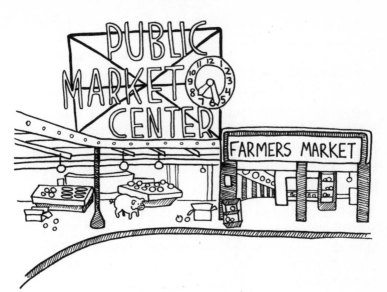

Pike Place Market

Scarce is the rural community, or city for that matter, that doesn't have at least one farmers' market where food producers, craftsmen and hobbyists gather to flog their wares. But for folks visiting or living in Seattle, a trip to the Pike Place Market provides patrons with a taste of Washington history along with their purchase.

A meager eight farmers towed wagons full of farm-fresh produce to the first market on August 17, 1907. Organizers may not have realized how prime a location the corner of First Avenue and Pike Street was, but long before the first day was out, they surely knew—by 11:00 AM, the farmers had sold out.

Of course, location wasn't the only draw. Price was definitely a factor as well. Apparently, the outrageous price of onions, with most of that money going to middlemen, so outraged citizens that Thomas Revell, a Seattle city councilman of the day, proposed and encouraged that first market. He argued that such a market would "connect farmers directly with consumers." It did, and with remarkable results.

Today, the Pike Place Market is open daily from 10:00 AM to 6:00 PM, attracting as many as 10 million visitors each year. What market began as a street-corner market has moved to Seattle's downtown and now occupies more than nine acres. And that first collection of eight farmers selling their wares is a thing of the past. Today, the Pike Place Market is home to 190 craftspeople and 120 farmers who rent table space by the day, 240 street performers and musicians and 300 apartments, (most of which house low-income elderly people), not to mention antique dealers, restaurants and even comic-book sellers.

Amazingly, it wasn't until the 1960s that the marketplace area was officially protected as a member of the National Register of Historic Places—and this only came about thanks to architect Victor Steinbrueck's activism against an urban renewal plan that would have taken out the heart of the structures and destroyed the market's history.

DID YOU  **KNOW?**

The Pike Place Market is known for its "flying fish." So much so, in fact, that they've found themselves the topic of an episode of the television sitcom *Frasier*, as well as being featured on the Learning Channel. Apparently, the "flying fish" scenario came about when employees of Pike Place Fish, one of the market's many vendors, decided that tossing the goods was faster than running from point A to point B and saved a lot of time. So if you're patronizing that outlet, remember to duck.

Starbucks Startup

The year: 1971. The location: the Pike Place Market. The product: none other than Starbucks coffee. That's right folks, the favorite brand of many a coffee lover and the biggest coffee chain in the world originated at this very location. And just a block away, you can still avail yourself of a cup of joe at the first Starbucks store to ever sell the bitter brew.

The International District

The Seattle International District has certainly earned its name, since it's the only place in the entire country where Chinese, Japanese, Filipino, Vietnamese, Korean, Laotian, Cambodian and other Asian Americans live in one neighborhood. It is located east of Interstate 5 and north of South Lane Street in an area of the city known as "Little Saigon."

Wing Lake Museum, Hing Hay Park, Kobe Terrace and Danny Woo Garden, one of the largest Asian markets in the U.S., are all located in Uwajimaya Village.

Experience Music Project

Hailed as a "rock and roll music museum with a difference," the Experience Music Project is a popular attraction for visitors and residents of Seattle alike. The museum was the brainchild of Paul Allen, a Microsoft entrepreneur looking for a way to honor the memory of super rock star Jimi Hendrix. While Hendrix is the main draw for visitors, an overview of American pop and rock music is also highlighted. Oh, and if you want to check it out, it's located at 325 Fifth Avenue North.

A Big Dam

If you're traveling along the Columbia River near Lake Roosevelt, make sure you stop to take a glimpse of the Grand Coulee Dam. It took nine years from the initial excavation of the site to the unveiling of the completed structure, but in 1941, it was hailed as the largest dam in the world. Water first flowed over the spillway on June 1, 1942.

Here are a few more facts about the Grand Coulee Dam:

☛ Although it is no longer the largest dam in the world, the Grand Coulee remains the largest concrete dam in North America and the largest concrete structure in the United States.

☞ The dam is 550 feet in height.

☞ The reservoir can hold 421 billion cubic feet of water.

☞ It takes four power plants and 33 generators to operate the dam.

☞ Grand Coulee is the largest hydroelectricity generator in the United States and the third largest in the world.

DID YOU  KNOW?

The Grand Coulee Dam was initially built to aid in the irrigation of desert areas and not for the production of electricity. But in 1941, when construction was completed and the world was engulfed in another world war, the dam was quickly put to use. It produced electricity for several wartime efforts, including aluminum smelting and the Manhattan Project—a top secret project focused on the development of nuclear weapons.

A Visit into Yesteryear

For those who like to reminisce about Washington's early beginnings, a trip to Ebey's Landing National Historical Reserve is well worth it. This national historic site is located on Whidbey Island. Congress founded it in 1978 in an effort to preserve one of the state's first rural communities, settled by Isaac Ebey in 1850. The historic village consists of two original forts, and visitors can learn about the development of the Puget Sound area from early exploration to the present day.

Gold Fever

It was a disease that affected its victims without discrimination. Some emerged intact but not unscathed. Others didn't make it out alive. For the select few who struck it rich, it remained debatable whether it was at all worthwhile. Still, it was an adventure that at the very least provided fodder for memories during one's golden years. And since 1996, the gold rush of 1897 has been commemorated by Klondike Gold Rush National Historical Park. The Seattle portion of the park is located in its Pioneer Square Historic District. But it doesn't stop there. In its entirety, the Klondike Gold Rush National Historic Park has sister sites in Skagway, Alaska, as well as the Canadian Chilkoot Trail National Historic Site in the Yukon and Dawson Historical Complex National Historic Site in Dawson City, Yukon.

Build It and They Will Come

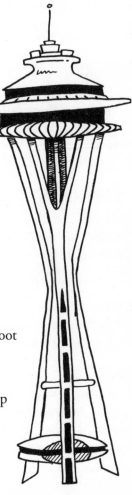

The Space Needle, originally called the "Space Cage," was built for the 1962 World's Fair. At the time, it was the tallest building west of the Mississippi River.

Now a Seattle icon, the Space Needle is privately owned and managed by the Space Needle Corporation. Here are a few quick facts about this must-see site:

- ☞ The idea to build the structure was the brainchild of artist Edward E. Carlson in 1959.

- ☞ It is situated on a 120-foot by 120-foot piece of land that cost investors $75,000 in 1961.

- ☞ The Space Needle has a 30-foot deep and 120-foot-wide underground concrete foundation that required 467 cement trucks to fill.

- The cement foundation weighs as much as the aboveground portion of the structure.

- The Space Needle is 605 feet high.

- An elevator can get you from the ground floor to the observation deck, 520 feet above, at a speed of 10 miles per hour or 14 feet per second. Do the math—you'll make it to your destination in less than 40 seconds.

- For fitter folk, there are 848 steps from top to bottom.

- The Space Needle cost $4.5 million to build.

- An aircraft warning beacon is fixed to the top of the structure.

- The Needle can withstand winds of 200 miles per hour and has withstood earthquake tremors measuring 6.8 on the Richter scale.

- The world's second-ever revolving restaurant, SkyCity (originally named "Eye of the Needle"), is housed in its UFO-shaped top.

- At least six daredevils have attempted to parachute off the Needle's heights.

- More than 20,000 people visit the Space Needle each day.

- It is touted as "Seattle's number one tourist destination."

DID YOU KNOW?

The movie *It Happened at the World's Fair* (1963), starring Elvis Presley, was filmed on site and features the Space Needle in many of its shots.

Historic Replica

If you've always wanted to visit England's Stonehenge but can't afford a transatlantic flight, why not head over to Maryhill. In 1930, lawyer, humanitarian and road builder Sam Hill built an exact replica on his property. Overlooking the town, the monument commemorates the soldiers who died in World War I. Hill began work on the project in 1918. He used concrete to build the huge structure and took his time to ensure as perfect a product as possible. In an odd twist of fate, Hill died shortly after his masterpiece was completed. His remains are buried at the site, and in an effort to restrict traffic, visitors must hike to the monument.

Today, the Maryhill Museum of Art maintains both Hill's Stonehenge and his mansion.

The Afterlife

There's nothing ghoulish about it. Really. Cemetery hopping is a perfectly acceptable pastime. In fact, the study of genealogy is considered one of the fastest-growing hobbies in North America. And what better places to dig up family secrets, as it were, than in a graveyard? Then imagine discovering a long-lost and forgotten graveyard with only a handful of graves. What a goldmine for family historians!

Chelan County boasts small and forgotten cemeteries, as well as a larger settlers' graveyard, and all surnames are indexed. Those interested in history and headstones should consider visiting:

☛ Blewett Cemetery

☛ the Lone Graves in the Peshastin Creek Drainage

☛ Brisky-Treadwell Cemetery

- Peshastin Cemetery

- Manson Indian Cemetery

- Chelan Fraternal Cemetery, the county's oldest such cemetery

DID YOU KNOW?

Among some of the more famous folk to find their final resting places in one of Seattle's graveyards are martial-arts film star Bruce Lee and his son, Brandon Lee; Jimi Hendrix; Princess Angeline, daughter of Chief Sealth (aka Chief Seattle); and Chief Sealth himself.

Animal Farm

Whether you've got a yearning to see a giraffe up close or want to check out what a Komodo dragon looks like, the Woodland Park Zoo has it all. Almost 300 animal species occupy the 92-acre zoo, which was established in Seattle in 1909. What makes this zoo unique is how it's divided into ecosystems and habitats specific to the animals housed in those areas. Over the years, the Woodland Park Zoo has been recognized with numerous awards from the American Zoo and Aquarium Association.

DID YOU KNOW?

The Tacoma Art Museum was founded in 1935 as the Tacoma Art Association and had four different homes before finally settling in at 1707 Pacific Avenue.

What's in a Name?

Located near Ilwaco, at the mouth of the Columbia River, the 53-foot-tall Cape Disappointment Lighthouse first shone its beacon of light onto a rough sea 200 feet beneath it on October 15, 1856. For lighthouse lovers, it's a sight not to be missed.

Columbia River Gorge

Located along the border of Washington and Oregon, the Columbia River runs through one of the state's most amazing natural wonders. The Columbia River Gorge measures 80 miles in length and is 4000 feet deep. The steep walls of the gorge create wind conditions that are ideal for windsurfing and sailing.

Snoqualmie Falls

First discovered by the Snoqualmie tribe, the magnificent 270-foot-high falls were named in their honor. Named with the Salish word for "moon," the Snoqualmie Falls captured the imagination of its first visitors, as it continues to do today, and the area is said to have inspired many a Native American legend.

Of course, anything of this magnificence is bound to tempt passing daredevils. Such was the case with Mr. Blondin. In 1889, following the festivities celebrating the arrival of the area's first passenger train, Blondin successfully walked a tightrope over the falls.

Charlie Anderson wasn't so lucky. Anderson decided to try parachuting into the canyon below the falls in 1890. Using a hot air balloon to get airborne, Anderson took his leap and released his chute. Gusting winds made landing difficult and he fell hard on the rocky floor of the canyon and died that night. One of Washington's most-visited sites, Snoqualmie Falls is just 29 miles from Seattle's city center.

A City Atop a City

What began as a localized fire started by a pot of overturned glue and fueled by neighboring wooden buildings (which included a hardware store equipped with ammo), soon became an explosive inferno. Thirty-three city blocks of what was referred to, in 1889, as downtown Seattle, were consumed in the blaze. But Washingtonians pride themselves in being of sturdy stock.

They're not the kind of folk to let disaster dictate their future, and they took to the task of rebuilding their business district almost immediately. In fact, the fire turned out to be a chance to rebuild in a better way.

BUILDING IT BETTER
Originally, the city center had been built on low, soft ground that frequently flooded. Following the fire, city officials proposed raising the street level by as much as 30 feet and building new buildings on top of old buildings in many cases. To sustain the raised business district, brick walls were built and reinforced with debris from the fire, garbage, soil—whatever was on hand. Eventually, a newcomer to the area wouldn't immediately have known the area had undergone such a change.

LIFE UNDERGROUND
Under the new structures, an eerie, underground community continued in a world without light. It was all very legitimate, at first. But over time, merchants found it unnecessary, even impractical, to continue using the lower levels of their buildings, and the area became a haven for the homeless and for illegal gambling houses and opium dens.

NEW RESTRICTIONS
Fear of an outbreak of bubonic plague put an end to any illegal inhabitation of the underground city in 1907, and city officials condemned the area and blocked access. It wasn't until 1965 that Seattle resident Bill Speidel had a brainstorm that he thought was definitely a win-win situation. The city of Seattle would get a little interesting PR, tourists would be intrigued, business owners would be compensated and Speidel would make a little money!

TOURIST DESTINATION
And so the idea of an underground tour was born. Today, a portion of the underground has been secured, and in many cases refurbished, and tours are conducted several times a day year round.

DID YOU KNOW?

Before Seattle's downtown district was completely rebuilt after the fire of 1889, pedestrians would occasionally find themselves climbing ladders from the sidewalk below to the new front door of the merchant where they wished to do business. As you can imagine, the ladies of the day, with their long, flowing skirts, must have found this humiliating. And there were reports of as many as 17 drunken fellas missing a rung and falling to their deaths.

Hidden Treasure

Not only does this site offer visitors a peek into the past, having been declared a state and national historic site, it gives visitors a chance to experience high-society late 19th-century style. While the ground was broken for the 10,000-square-foot, 20-room mansion known as "Hoquiam's Castle" back in 1897 by lumber baron Robert Lytle, the Washington landmark wasn't completed until 1900. But while the architectural brilliance of Hoquiam's Castle was featured in National Geographic's *America's Great Houses*, it actually sat empty and abandoned for many years after the death of Lytle's niece, Theadosia Bale, in the late 1950s. Purchased in 1968 by the Watson family, a continuous restoration began that continues to this day. Currently, the castle is owned by Donna Grow. And for as little as $145, you too can experience a night in an historic castle whose walls must contain a plethora of stories.

DID YOU KNOW?

The town of Startup is a small community of less than 1000 inhabitants, based on the 2000 census. Named after lumber company manager George G. Startup, it is also coincidentally the location where "visitors start up into the mountain."

Beacon Rock State Park

If you're an avid mountain climber, this park is likely the destination of your dreams. Located 35 miles east of Vancouver, the northwest face of this 4650-acre park is open for technical climbing all year. The south and southeast faces are closed to climbing from February 1 through July 15 each year, and the east face is closed year round because of "environmental sensitivity." The rest of the park is open from April 1 to October 18 and features camping, hiking and water-related activities. Of particular interest to visitors is the fact that the park is actually the core of an ancient volcano. As well, walking trails provide particularly amazing views of the Columbia River Gorge.

Ye Olde Curiosity Shop

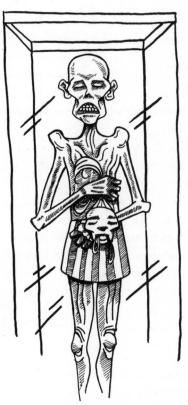

If you're into the madly macabre and oddly absurd, Seattle's famed Ye Olde Curiosity Shop is a must-see stop. Located on the waterfront, the tourist attraction boasts a collection of authentic Northwest and Alaskan art, along with a mummy nicknamed Sylvester, a collection of shrunken heads from Ecuador, a two-headed calf and a mermaid. Established by Ohio-native Joseph E. "Daddy" Standley in 1899, the shop first gained recognition for its worldly collection of oddities during the Yukon Gold Rush, and it continues to draw both visitors and residents alike.

Clams Galore!

If you're visiting any of the natural beaches of Puget Sound and Washington's ocean coastline, taking part in a family clam dig is nothing short of a rite of passage. It's simple, really. Just get everyone together, supply each person with a shovel and pail—toy versions are perfectly acceptable—and get digging.

Clams aren't stupid, so prepare yourself to dig deep—sometimes two or three feet down—before you snag your first clam or two. As soon as they know you're fishing for their innards, they'll skooch away—yes, they can swim in the soft sand. But if you're quick enough, you'll likely be able to snag the ingredients for a seaside clam chowder to die for! Just snap the shells open, pull out the insides, stoke the fire and start cooking!

Other Sandy Treasures

If clams aren't your thing, how about digging for bottles?
Apparently the shores along Washington's coastline are known
to be a bottle hunter's dream. In earlier days, bottles came in an
assortment of shapes and sizes, and many were lost or discarded
and became buried in the sandy shoreline, hidden underneath
docks or even tangled up in beaver damns. And don't think
well-traveled areas aren't likely to conceal a few treasures.
A Chinese pot was uncovered in an empty lot in Egmont, and
another collector unearthed an old beer bottle in a beaver dam.

FESTIVALS

A Selection of Celebrations

The following festivals and events represent a selected list culled from a variety of sources. There is much more happening should you be inclined to look further!

Skagit Valley Tulip Festival, Skagit Valley

The Skagit Valley Tulip Festival, which began in 1983, is held annually during the month of April. Thousands of tulips grow in this western Washington valley, and events surrounding their blooming occur throughout April to entertain the 500,000-plus tourists who come to ogle.

How did the festival get its start? In 1947, William Roozen moved to Washington from Holland and turned his background in tulip growing to good use by starting a small tulip-growing company and expanding it year after year. In 1955, Roozen bought Washington's original tulip supplier—still known as the Washington Bulb Company—and it is still run by the Roozen family today. The family is the largest grower of tulips, daffodils and irises in the United States, and they use the majority of their 2000 acres of farmland to grow them.

The Skagit Valley leads the tulip industry in North America. The Washington Bulb Company sells over 50 million tulip stems every year, along with millions of bulbs.

Manson Apple Blossom Festival, Manson

The Manson Apple Blossom Festival is held annually during the second weekend of May. The first Apple Blossom Festival was held in 1921, in a pavilion built over the water. A Royalty Pageant started in 1928 and continues today. Other festival activities include Nostalgia Night, the Edible Apple Contest, a fun run, the Kiwanis breakfast, a quilt show, parade, craft and food fair, a Chicken Noodle Dinner, a student art show, a car and Harley show, a rock and mineral show and much more.

Sequim Lavender Festival, Sequim

The Sequim Lavender Festival began in 1996 and is held annually on the third weekend of July. The scent-laden fest typically draws over 30,000 people from around the world. Part of the fest includes a street fair in downtown Sequim, which typically hosts about 150 craftspeople and lavender vendors, as well as music, food and wine tasting. Eight lavender farms host field tours and herb-centered activities, demonstrations, music and food.

The valley of Sequim is home to about 40 lavender farms, in part because of the excellent growing conditions. Sequim is in what is called a "rain shadow"—essentially a rain umbrella provided by the Olympic Mountains, which shields it from the overly abundant rain that falls to the east and west. The geography also provides the sunniest weather in western Washington and temperatures that only vary about 20 degrees from day to night, so the plants are never shocked by extreme temperature changes and can thrive.

DID YOU KNOW?

Sequim is the lavender capital of North America.

National Lentil Festival, Pullman

Since 1983, Pullman's Lentil Festival has been held each August. The event provides free lentil chili, a grand parade, food, arts and crafts, live music, a kids' area and stage, a lentil cook-off, a beer garden and several sporting activities to boot.

In case you didn't know, lentils are highly nutritious legumes (beans are also legumes and are related to lentils). In fact, just a cup of cooked lentils contains 90 percent of the recommended daily allowance (RDA) of folic acid, making them the number one folic acid–containing food (unfortified food, that is). Lentils help the body absorb iron, provide protein and have been shown to help lower cholesterol levels, too!

DID YOU KNOW?

Pullman is in the Palouse region of Washington and the area's farmers grow one-third of the lentils produced in the United States annually. They are known for producing the highest quality lentils in the world. How much might one-third of the lentils grown in the U.S. be? Approximately 150 million pounds each year!

Washington State International Kite Festival, Long Beach
The Washington State International Kite Festival is held on the third full week of August and celebrated its 25th anniversary in 2006.

The festival was voted the "Best Kite Festival in the World" by the Kite Trade Association International, and it attracts famous

kite fliers from all over the globe, many who put on choreo-graphed shows for the tens of thousands of tourists that attend.

Long Beach is also home to the World Kite Museum and Hall of Fame—the only museum in America dedicated to the kite.

It turns out that Long Beach is aptly named, as it is the longest natural beach in the U.S., measuring 28 miles in length.

Seafair, Seattle

Seafair is an annual event held July through August in Seattle. The festival kicks off each year with a landing on Alki Beach by the "Seafair Pirates," a group of Seattle goodwill ambassadors who dress in pirate costumes and disembark from a ship to frolic on the beach, much to the delight of local children and visiting tourists. The first Pirates were members of the Washington State Press Club, who conceived the Seafair festival idea in 1949 and produced the first one in 1950.

The Seafair festival culminates with a hydroplane race on Lake Washington, complete with an aerial show provided by the U.S. Navy's Blue Angels. In between, a plethora of events takes place, including the Green Lake Milk Carton Derby and the Torchlight Parade. The Torchlight Parade is a large affair that draws a few hundred thousand people each year and includes participants from around the globe. In fact, it is the largest parade in the Northwest and one of the top 10 largest parades in the United States.

DID YOU KNOW?

The first Seafair in 1950 was designed to attract tourists. It was called "Seafair" because of Seattle's long-time claim to being the "Boating Capital of the World" (Seattle has more pleasure boats per capita than anywhere else in the U.S.).

An Aqua Theater seating 5000 was built at Green Lake, and the Aqua Follies were born. The Follies included a diving show, 30 synchronized female swimmers and 24 ballet dancers. There were nightly shows as well as midnight matinees, and famous personalities such as Bob Hope and Olympic divers performed there over the years. The theater was used for plays and musicals outside of Seafair and was a key forum for the 1962 World's Fair.

After the World's Fair, the site's usage dropped significantly, the grandstand fell into disrepair, and it was largely dismantled in 1970. Today, part of the old grandstand houses crew boats (also known as shells, sweep boats and sculling boats).

A Taste of Edmonds, Edmonds

A Taste of Edmonds, Snohomish County's largest festival, is held annually on the second weekend in August. About 100,000 people attend the three-day weekend event, which includes fine arts and crafts, about 40 food vendors, over four stages of entertainment, as well as rides and beer and wine gardens. This festival was voted one of the top 100 in North America!

The Bite of Seattle, Seattle

The Bite of Seattle is one of Seattle's biggest festivals, occurring every July. The event was started in 1982 by Alan Silverman, president of Festivals, Inc., who wanted to recognize the amazing chefs that call the city home. The first Bite of Seattle took place at Greenlake, a relatively small outdoor space that played host to almost 75,000 attendees and 25 restaurants. By 1986, the festival had outgrown the Greenlake location and moved to the grounds of Seattle Center. Today the event draws nearly half a million people over a three-day weekend, providing "bites" of food from more than 60 local restaurants and allowing both residents and tourists to get a small and affordable taste of what various restaurants offer.

Some factoids on the Bite:

- Over 3.5 miles of gas pipe are laid down for cooking at the event.

- The food preparation uses 2000 gallons of hot water.

- To keep things cool, 715,000 pounds of ice are required.

- An average of 12,000 gallons of soda pop are served.

- Festival patrons inbibe about 365 kegs of beer.

Westport Art Festival, Westport

Since 1998, the Westport Art Festival has been held annually in August. The juried arts and crafts event centers on local art and artisans. In addition to artists' wares on display, entertainment includes music, clowns, stilt walkers and magicians.

DID YOU KNOW?

Westport has the largest marina on the Washington coast. It is known as the "Salmon Capital of the World" and is famous for its deep-sea fishing.

Grays Harbor is home to the Grays Harbor Lighthouse, which at 107 feet is the tallest in the state and the second tallest on the entire West Coast.

Wahkiakum County Fair, Skamokawa

The Wahkiakum County Fair, which got its start in 1909, is an annual event that occurs on the fourth Thursday, Friday and Saturday in August. The county itself is the third smallest in the state but contains many historical sites within its boundaries. For example, there are eight marked Lewis and Clark expedition heritage sites.

DID YOU KNOW?

Wahkiakum County was named for a Native American village on the Columbia River.

Finn-Fest USA, Naselle

Since the early 1980s, Finn-Fest has been held every other year in the summer in the town of Naselle. This Finnish-American folk festival celebrates Finnish food, music, traditional dance, dress, games and more. Naselle was settled by Finns in the mid-1800s and still has a large Finnish population, making this festival a natural for the town.

Covered Bridge Festival, Grays River

The annual Covered Bridge Festival in Grays River, which began in 2005, is a recent addition to the area. The event includes music, games, dancing, a beer garden, an antique parade and a fun run!

Why have a bridge as a festival theme? The Grays River Covered Bridge happens to be the oldest covered bridge in the Northwest. Built in 1905, it was covered in 1908. The bridge is 158 feet long and is listed on the National Register of Historic Places.

Bumbershoot, Seattle

Bumbershoot is an annual Seattle event held every Labor Day weekend. The festival takes its name from a colloquial word for umbrella, and it's usually assumed that the name was chosen because of Seattle's famous drizzly weather. In actuality, the name is a metaphor for the variety of arts that the event brings together under "one chute."

The festival is the largest international music and arts festival in North America and celebrates a rainbow of artistic disciplines and genres.

DID YOU KNOW?

In 1971, Bumbershoot's inaugural year, the festival included a "Miss Hot Pants Contest," an amateur motorcycle race, an over-size-inflatable-sculpture contest and body painting. Ahhh, those 1970s. Needless to say, many of the events have changed over the years—no more "Miss Hot Pants."

Harbor Days, Olympia

This annual Labor Day weekend event celebrates the South Sound's maritime heritage and brings together vintage, working and retired tugboats, many which come to moor at Olympia's Percival Landing for the festival. Tugboat races based on engine size are a Harbor Days highlight, but the event also provides a display of model tugboats and a variety of arts and crafts vendors.

Ellensburg Rodeo, Ellensburg

The Ellensburg Rodeo is another annual Labor Day event. Riders, ropers, and wrestlers compete in the arena for $250,000 in prize money.

The first official Ellensburg Rodeo took place in 1923, inspired by a local rodeo put on by the Ferguson family, and it continued to grow and gain popularity with the local cowboys working the cattle ranches. The family helped the city set up the event, and it has become one of the largest professional rodeos in the United States.

DID YOU KNOW?

The Ellensburg Rodeo is considered one of America's top 25 professional rodeos and draws over 500 contestants each year.

Valleyfest, Spokane Valley

Since 1990, Spokane Valley's Valleyfest has been held annually each September. The Fest takes place in Mirabeau Park in the Spokane Valley and includes a fun run, parade and a variety of entertainment. Its goal is to recognize the youth of the city and bring families and neighbors together.

The Great Prosser Balloon Rally, Prosser

The Great Prosser Balloon Rally is an annual event held during the fourth full weekend of September. The rally includes balloon launches, the Night Glow Show, a harvest festival, a farmers' market and the Caren Mercer-Andreason Street Painting Festival.

The Prosser Balloon Rally got its start in 1989 thanks to balloon pilot Ted Wirchs' in-laws. The story goes that Ted came into town and provided his in-laws with a ride. He was struck by the beauty of the place and decided to create an annual event for fellow balloon enthusiasts.

Apple Days, Cashmere

Cashmere celebrates Apple Days annually during the first weekend of October. The festivities mark the end of the apple harvest each fall and include vendors, magicians, musicians and "shoot-outs" between the sheriff and saloon "robbers." As Cashmere is built on part of the Oregon Trail, the Oregon Trail Travelers visit the Apple Days event every year, setting up tents and showing festival attendees what life was like on the trail.

The town of Cashmere is at the exact center of the state and has a couple of famous sites, including the Pioneer Village, which consists of 20 original pioneer structures dating back to the late 1800s and the Liberty Orchards (Aplets & Cotlets) candy factory.

Wings and Wheels Festival

The Wings and Wheels Festival got its start in 2002 and is held annually on the first weekend of October. It features a classic car show, a motorcycle show, a parade, an airport fly-in and lots of food and entertainment.

The festival commemorates the first nonstop flight across the Pacific Ocean by Clyde Pangborn, from Bridgeport, and Hugh Herndon Jr. They flew from Misawa, Japan, to Wenatchee and landed successfully on October 5, 1931. The 5000-mile flight took 41 hours and 15 minutes. At the time, Pangborn was already a famous aviator, having flown in the U.S. army during World War I. He went on to become a well-known "barnstormer" (aerial stuntman) in the 1920s.

DID YOU KNOW?

Pangborn and Herndon's Pacific crossing was almost double the distance that Charles Lindbergh flew across the Atlantic four years earlier. In fact, a feat equal or greater to the Pacific crossing wasn't replicated for 30 years, when jet airliners came onto the scene.

Dungeness Crab and Seafood Festival, Port Angeles

The Dungeness Crab and Seafood Festival is an annual early fall event. The Dungeness crab is considered a delicacy for its size and mild, sweet flavor. Rather than the town being named after the crab, the crab—in this case—

was named after the town of Dungeness, which is in the Port Angeles area. The festival includes food, cooking demonstrations, crafts, wine and beer, fine arts and music.

The Dungeness Crab and Seafood Festival organizers donate a portion of the proceeds to watershed education in Dungeness River and Bay habitats and other environmental issues that affect the local aquiculture/ agriculture.

Christmas Lighting Festival, Leavenworth

Leavenworth's annual Christmas Lighting Festival started in 1969. On December Fridays before Christmas, the town waits in darkness for Saturday's lighting festivities, when everyone gathers at the Gazebo to greet Saint Nicholas. Other festival activities include roasting chestnuts, holiday music, sledding and sleigh rides. At dusk, everyone gathers to sing "Silent Night" and witness the lighting of the village and park.

DID YOU KNOW?

The A&E Network named Leavenworth the "Ultimate Holiday Town USA" in 2003.

WEIRD AND SPOOKY

Sparky the Friendly Ghost

The Capitol Theatre in Yakima is a renovated vaudeville play-house from the 1920s that evolved first into a movie theater, then a community arts center. Special, *ghostly* community member "Sparky" has been known to adjust the lighting and shuffle items around, much to the chagrin of the stage manager. He is, however, credited with once saving a girl's life.

Constant Police Presence

Worried about bar fights? Perhaps you should drink your next brew at the old Oxford Tavern in Snohomish—where the ghost of a former policeman named Henry is said to still patrol. If you don't manage to catch a glimpse of him, you can take a look at his photograph, which still hangs on the wall.

Victorian Ghosts in Port Townsend

The town of Port Townsend contains several buildings thought to be haunted. One of the most popular and well known is Manresa Castle, which now functions as a hotel. Two rooms of the castle are particularly famous: room 302, the turret room below the attic in which a priest hanged himself, and room 306, where a young woman named Kate, a visitor when the house was a private residence, allegedly threw herself out a window after learning her fiancé had been lost at sea.

Of Stephen King Lore

In 2002, ABC-TV helped make history in Lakewood by using the famed Thornewood Castle as a film location.

Work on the 31,000-square-foot "home" began in 1908 and took four years to complete. The finished project cost Chester Thorne a cool $1 million—a substantial but not overwhelming amount for the successful owner of the National Bank of Commerce.

New owner and resort developer Steve Redwine began restorative work on the castle in 1980, and work continued under new owners Richard and Debbie Mirau in 1995, and finally Deanna and Wayne Robinson in 2000. Today, visitors can visit the past when they book a night's stay at the stately 40-room mansion. And in 2001, ABC/Disney chose the location as the setting for the haunted mansion in the three-part miniseries *Rose Red*, penned by Stephen King.

Ghostly Tales of the Northwest

Like any other longstanding community fixture, the Burnley School of Professional Art, now more commonly known as the Art Institute of Seattle, has at least one skeleton in its closet— or rather, a ghostly past to deal with.

First established by Edwin and Elsie Burnley in 1946, the school got off to a rather uneventful start. It wasn't until the business changed hands, after it was bought by Jess Cauthorn in 1960, that students started reporting odd incidents and disturbing encounters. Staff and students would frequently be greeted in the morning with rearranged classrooms. Footsteps were heard making their way down unoccupied hallways.

One unconfirmed urban legend points to the accidental death of a high school student, which supposedly occurred just a few years before the school was sold, as the cause of the unsettling disturbances, though the ghostly occupant didn't seem to mind sharing the space with its more earthly inhabitants.

In 1985, the school moved to another location. According to at least one source, staff and students no longer report odd happenings. In fact, the school's official website doesn't even mention its ghostly past—curious, considering it's great fodder for the creative mind!

Other Ghostly Encounters

If you're venturing through the University of Washington's College Inn Pub, don't be too surprised to spot an old man dressed in a khaki trench coat who knocks back ghostly beers. Apparently the fellow, lovingly named Howard, is a regular there.

Flying Saucers Have a Special Affinity for Washington

The first reported sighting of a UFO occurred near Mt. Rainier on June 24, 1947. A pilot named Kenneth Arnold saw nine flying disks—reports of which led to the coining of the term "flying saucers"—in a chain formation, traveling at what he estimated to be about 1200 miles per hour (significantly faster than any military planes were capable of traveling at the time). To date, an unusual number of UFOs are spotted regularly in the Trout Lake area near Mt. Adams. In fact, James Gilliland of Gilliland Ranch has been host to many visitors who come to witness the unexplained phenomenon.

The Case of the Mysterious Windshield Pitting

Strange "pits" started appearing on windshields all over the west side of Washington State simultaneously in the spring of 1954, and panic rippled through citizens. Theorized causes ran the gamut and included radio signals gone awry, cosmic ray damage from the sun, supersonic sound waves, nuclear bomb testing fallout—even gremlins were thought to be the possible cause! Small pockmarks in automobile windshields were first reported in Bellingham, and then the phenomenon began traveling south—first to Sedro-Wooley, then Mount Vernon, Anacortes, Whidbey Island and finally Seattle.

Police were stumped. The Marines stationed on Whidbey performed intensive searches. The governor asked University of Washington scientists to investigate, and what they came back with...well, it was less than satisfactory. They said the reports over-emphasized the pitting, and they believed that people simply hadn't noticed it until it was brought to their attention.

After further investigation by police, working off this new idea, it was determined that this was actually a case of "collective delusion," and the incident has become a classic in psychology classrooms. Max Allison of the Seattle police crime lab gave a statement saying that the problem was a result of "five percent hoodlum-ism and 95 percent public hysteria." Pitting reports ended in mid-April 1954 and haven't returned since. Perhaps you haven't checked your windshield?

Snohomish County Ghost Towns

MONTE CRISTO

While the bulk of mining in Washington was done in the eastern part of the state, Snohomish County in the west had its fair share of mining settlements. Monte Cristo was the largest, and in the late 1800s, the town—ringed by peaks high in the Cascade mountain range—had 2000 residents. By the turn of the 20th century, the settlement began going bankrupt, and today, no one lives in this remote location. The railroad is also long gone. Regardless, some cabins, active claims and the

remains of a concentrator, powerhouse and mill can still be seen at the site. Should you feel adventurous, the town is a four-mile hike from Barlow Pass off the Mountain Loop Highway. Note that the newer cabins on site do not indicate ghosts at work; rather, they belong to the Forest Service.

SILVERTON

Silverton was a slightly larger mining town just west of Monte Cristo. Also founded in the 1890s, it was once home to over 2500 people. It's located right on the Mountain Loop Highway, just 20 miles east of Granite Falls. A visit today would yield you some well-kept private homes mostly used for vacationing, a millpond, mine shafts, old tram cables and rusting mine carts.

GALENA AND MINERAL CITY

Two more mining towns—Galena and Mineral City—were in close proximity to Monte Cristo and Silverton; reaching them today is best done off Forest Road 63, nine miles north of Index, where one can hike into Mineral City from where the north fork of the Skykomish River meets Silver Creek. This juncture is, in fact, where Galena used to be. Mineral City was once a good-sized town, encompassing 15 city blocks complete with stores, saloons and hotels. As a railroad into town was never built and the mines failed, the inhabitants all fled. All you can see now on the site are old mine shafts, roads and bridges—all the structures have disappeared.

HOW THE WEST WAS WON

The First Settlers

Most of the non-Native population settled on the west side of the state near bodies of water, primarily Puget Sound, Willapa Harbor and along the Columbia River. This was in part because eastern Washington was "closed" to settlement in the mid-1850s because of warring Native tribes.

There's Gold in Them There Hills

Once eastern Washington "re-opened" for settlement in the late 1850s, gold and silver were discovered and created a boom in the area, which included northeast Washington and north Idaho. Walla Walla was at the heart of this boom and became the county seat east of the mountains.

The Klondike Gold Rush in Canada was a huge contributor to the growth of Washington, particularly Seattle. The madness started after the steamship *Portland* docked with 68 miners and a two tons of gold. Word spread, and soon people from all over the country and the world were coming through Seattle to board ships bound for Alaska—the route to Canada's Klondike region. Rate wars broke out and ticket prices climbed outrageously. People were paying upwards of $1500 for a ticket that didn't even guarantee a bed on board.

DID YOU KNOW?

In July 1898, an assay office was set up in Seattle to test and weigh the gold of returning miners. Over $15 million worth of gold was assayed in the first 14 months.

Washington Becomes Official

On November 11, 1889, Washington was officially granted statehood and became a member of the Union. By this time, the population had exploded from an original 4000 when it initially became a territory in 1853 to more than 300,000 when it joined the Union. Seattle was the largest of the settled regions and boasted approximately 40,000 residents. At this point in the state's history, the majority of leaders were of the Republication party, which had been true since the Civil War.

FOUNDING FATHERS

A New Territory Is Born

The current State of Washington was once part of the Oregon Territory, which was created in 1846 and included lands from California to Canada and from the Rockies to the Pacific Ocean. Oregon City was the seat of government until 1851, when Salem was given the honor. As the territory Salem governed was enormous, dissatisfaction by constituents shortly ensued. In 1853, a separate Washington Territory was created and included some of what today is Idaho and Montana.

Arthur Armstrong Denny (1822–99)

Considered the founder of Seattle, Denny was fascinated by stories of the Oregon wilderness and convinced his young family to come west from Illinois with him. When he arrived in Oregon, he sent others ahead to Puget Sound to explore first, as his wife and youngest baby had fallen ill. News back was positive, and he then hired a schooner to take his party of 24 to Elliott Bay. On November 13, 1851, they landed at Alki Point. Denny and his party quickly staked claims—and the streets surrounding those properties still bear their names. David Denny, Arthur's brother, claimed land that in part is the Denny Way of today. William Bell, who met the Dennys in Portland, claimed the area we now call Belltown. Arthur Denny and his brother-in-law Carson Boren claimed land that is now the commercial epicenter of the city.

Denny began doing business with the ships that came for lumber; the vessels would bring merchandise to sell or trade, and Denny arranged to take what was left and sell it for them on commission. It was a sort of wholesale agreement that he eventually turned into a general store, in partnership with Dexter Horton and David Phillips. Their shop was on the corner of Commercial (now First Avenue South) and Washington Street.

Henry Yesler (1810–92)

Yesler arrived in Elliott Bay in October 1852, coming to Seattle with the goal of opening a steam sawmill. The existing founders adjusted their claims and allowed Yesler to take the area at the foot of what was called Mill Street but what we know today as Yesler Way. This road is considered to be the original "skid road," as logs had to be dragged across it by oxen to get to the mill. Yesler and his wife first lived in a house across from the mill at the end of James Street, but the house was destroyed in the Great Seattle Fire of 1889. The house was replaced with another one, which is known today as the Pioneer Building—an office building still in use. Yesler later built a mansion at Fourth and Yesler, the later site of the Yesler Building that today is home to the King County offices. Yesler's wife Sarah was the city's first librarian and spent time volunteering and helping less fortunate women.

David "Doc" Maynard (1808–73)

Maynard arrived on the heels of the Denny party in April 1852 and claimed a waterfront site known today as Pioneer Square. He built a home at the northwest corner of First Avenue South and Main Street and opened a storefront in the house. Maynard provided the first logs to Yesler's mill when it opened. He had come to Seattle on the advice of his friend, Chief Sealth, whom he had met in Olympia, where he had settled first. It was Doc who suggested that the city be named for the chief.

Maynard was known as a kind man who put others' needs ahead of his own. He founded Seattle's first hospital, acting as physician while his wife served as nurse. He was the first person to be buried at Lakeview Cemetery.

John "Iron Man of the Hoh" Huelsdonk (1866–1946)

Huelsdonk and his wife, Dora, were the first white settlers to make a property claim on the Olympic Peninsula in 1891. The "Iron Man" legend came out of the fact that he was a very strong man who often packed loads weighing 150 to 200 pounds up trails to workers needing provisions. The rumors became distorted over time and both the nickname and the stories grew. He was also famous for being an incredibly skilled and brave hunter and trapper, killing at least—per his own estimation— 150 cougars *and* as many bears. In fact, in 1933, Huelsdonk was attacked by a bear while on fire patrol on the Snahapish River. He fought back so ferociously that he managed to not only escape what for most would have been certain death, but he also shot and killed the bear! He then walked five miles home and refused to see the doctor. When his wife made it clear he had to seek medical help, he capitulated and walked 17 miles to the nearest hospital in Forks. He was kept there for three weeks after getting 32 stitches and many a bandage. Another famous feat Huelsdonk performed in 1936 was killing the largest cougar ever seen on the peninsula. The cat had been terrorizing area farmers by killing their livestock and was nicknamed "Big Foot" because of the enormous tracks it left. Huelsdonk tracked the animal and shot it out of a tree. It measured over 11 feet from its nose to the tip of its tail! The Huelsdonk Homestead was listed on the Washington Heritage Register as an historic place in 1972.

DID YOU KNOW?

The Hoh Valley (which encompasses the Hoh Rain Forest) is considered to be the wettest area in the continental United States, earning the distinction by providing an annual 12 feet of rain to the lush vegetation it houses.

Thomas Mercer (1813–98)

Mercer led a party towards Seattle that included John Bagley, Dexter Horton and his brother, Aaron Mercer. Thomas Mercer first came alone to Seattle in the spring of 1852, claiming land at the foot of Queen Anne Hill (now known as Mercer Street). He then returned to Oregon and brought the rest of the party to Seattle in the spring of 1853. Mercer was Seattle's first teamster and milkman and was responsible for naming the most famous lakes in the area because of a speech he gave to guests one July 4. He suggested the large lake (now Lake Washington) be named for George Washington and the smaller lake, which he theorized might end up connecting Lake Washington to Puget Sound, be named Lake Union. Mercer Island, in the middle of Lake Washington, was named after Thomas Mercer.

Washington's First Governor

Isaac Stevens (1818–62) was the first governor of the newly created Washington Territory, appointed by President Franklin Pierce in 1853. He arrived in the territory the following year and declared January 30, 1854, as the date for election of the first legislative assembly.

The population of the new territory was sparse, estimated to include about 4000 non-Natives. Of that number, 1600 men cast their votes for who would represent them in the legislature. The average age of the newly elected officials was 28 years old. Ten were farmers, seven were lawyers and four were mechanics, with no other occupations represented by more than one member. Members were paid $3 per day, along with considerable amounts of whiskey. During the elections, a delegate to Congress was also chosen. The Democrats were the majority elected, with Whigs in the extreme minority. The Republican party was still two years away from being created.

Governor Stevens was also named the Superintendent of Indian Affairs, and he was in command of the northern route survey for the proposed transcontinental railroad. His true legacy was in regard to aboriginal affairs. He was responsible for creating the first Native land reservations by gathering various tribes together in a treaty council, which ultimately approved Stevens' plan. In addition to land, the agreements included schools, services and health care for Native Americans. Unfortunately, though, the reality of the plan was different than either side had intended, largely because of cultural misunderstandings and government decisions that occurred after Stevens' reign. The Natives did not end up receiving anything close to what they had been promised.

Seattle's Namesake

Chief Noah Sealth (1786–1866) came to a treaty agreement with Governor Isaac Stevens. He was named chief of the Allied Tribes of Puget Sound by Stevens and ensured the peaceful acceptance of his tribes. He was greatly respected by town leaders, and the city was named in his honor—the English pronunciation of Sealth being "Seattle."

A memorial statue of Chief Sealth, originally unveiled on Founder's Day, November 13, 1912, stands on Tilikum Place at Fifth Avenue and Denny Way. It was listed on the National Register of Historic Places in 1984.

Chief Sealth's Speech

"How can you buy or sell the sky, the warmth of the land? The idea is strange to us. If we do not own the freshness of the air and the sparkle of the water, how can you buy them?"

Many may recognize this as one of many often-quoted lines from Chief Sealth's famous speech of 1854, but few likely realize that there are a number of questions surrounding the authenticity of these words.

The chief's historic speech was in direct response to an offer by Territorial Governor Isaac Stevens. The governor wanted to purchase the land that Chief Sealth and his people occupied—two million acres—for a lump sum of $150,000.

TIME GAP

The chief's famous speech, entitled "Seattle's Reply" in the *Seattle Sunday Star*, was recorded by Dr. Henry A. Smith and wasn't printed until 1887, more than 30 years later. And since the chief's mother tongue was Lushootseed, and there were no concrete records to indicate what kind of translation may have taken place at the time, Smith's claim that these were, indeed, Chief Sealth's words, cannot be confirmed.

To gum up the issue even more, several other versions of the speech have circulated over the years, including a version written by scriptwriter Ted Perry that was later used in a 1972 film called *Home*.

TIMELESS MESSAGE

Still, regardless of their authenticity, these poetic words continue to stand as a monument to the belief of North America's indigenous peoples.

The gravestone marking Chief Sealth's final resting place displays a significant historical epitaph: "Firm Friend of the Whites, and For Him the City of Seattle was Named by Its Founders."

Early African American Presence in Society

John T. Gayton (1866–1954) came to Seattle in 1887, worked at a variety of jobs and studied in the evenings. In August 1933, President Franklin D. Roosevelt appointed him U.S. District Court Librarian—a position he held for 20 years. He and his family were pillars of the community, and his family's social outings were often reported in the local *Seattle Republican* paper.

Legislation allowing women to vote in Washington was first proposed by Arthur A. Denny in 1854. Were it not for one vote, it would have passed! That one vote holdout, however, was for an honorable reason. It turns out that the proposed ruling would only have allowed white women to participate, and the man who voted against the proposition was married to a Native woman and believed that she and her people should be included.

Early Lawmaker

Elwood Evans (d. 1898) was involved in politics from the time he was a clerk at the first legislative meeting in 1854. Evans was House Speaker in 1875 and later became a member of the first State House in 1889. Further, he was Territorial Secretary during the Civil War. Also the first president of the State Bar Association, he had a large impact on Washington's formation because he was actively involved in the codification of territorial laws.

Joshua Green (1869–1975)

Honored as the "Man of the Century," the state proclaimed his 100th birthday in 1969 as "Joshua Green Day." Green was president of the largest steamboat company on Puget Sound.

WOMEN WHO RATTLED WASHINGTON

Bertha Knight Landes (1868–1943)

Bertha Knight Landes achieved it a first for women not only in Washington, but across North America when she was elected mayor of Seattle in 1926. It was the first time a woman had been elected to such a prestigious post in a major American city, and she accomplished this feat with her platform of "municipal housekeeping." But devoting energy to a mayoralty campaign and coming up with a snappy-sounding motto weren't the only reasons she earned her title. Bertha Knight Landes was a hard-working, community activist whose ongoing leadership roles in organizations such as the Women's Auxiliary of University Congregational Church and the league of Women Voters earned her considerable recognition.

Dr. Blanche Sellers Lavizzo (1925–84)

Blanche Sellers Lavizzo arrived in Seattle in July 1956, credentials in hand and ready to be the first African American woman to establish herself as a pediatrician in the state. In 1970, she furthered her modest private practice by becoming the first medical director of the Odessa Brown Children's Clinic, leaving a permanent mark on the facility with her development of the clinic's motto "Quality care with dignity." In her honor, Yesler Atlantic Pedestrian Pathway was renamed Dr. Blanche Lavizzo Park in 1991.

Clara McCarty (1858–1929)

In 1880, at the tender age of 20 years, Clara McCarty was elected superintendent of Pierce County schools. Not only was she the first woman in the county to win elective office, she did so three years before women were even granted the right to vote in Washington.

Emma Smith DeVoe (1848–1927)

Emma Smith DeVoe was one of the main reasons Washington was the fifth state to grant voting rights to women. President of the Washington Equal Suffrage Association, she was considered a major figure in the American women's suffrage movement and a Republican Party activist. Her contributions were significant in making Washington the first state in the Pacific Northwest that allowed women to vote in 1910. Emma DeVoe didn't stop with acquiring rights for Washington women, but continued her efforts until 1920, when the vote was granted to all American women.

DID YOU KNOW?

Susan B. Anthony addressed the House of Representatives in Washington on October 19, 1871, regarding women's suffrage. It was the first time a woman had addressed a legislative body in the U.S.

Lou Graham (1861–1903)

Thought by many to be one of the most powerful women in Seattle's history, Lou Graham added an interesting twist to "liberating" women back in that city's early years. Born Dorothea Georgine Emile Ohben, Graham arrived in Seattle from Germany in 1888 and almost immediately set out to tempt city leaders with an interesting business proposal—to open an aboveboard brothel. Now, this wouldn't be just any old henhouse. Oh no, her girls would be intelligent, talented and beautiful; they'd be housed in a building comparable to any of the city's finest hotels; and prices for services rendered would be clearly posted. One can only guess the manner of her persuasion, since in short order she'd purchased a property on the corner of Third and Washington and was open for business. Her first place of business went up in flames in the Great Seattle Fire of June 6, 1889, but that was no problem. She'd already accumulated enough profit to build a new, stone building. The business served drinks and provided all manner of pleasures, which curiously enough, were "all free to government representatives."

MAVERICK MEN

Walter Vernon Lawson (1926–82)

It wasn't until July 1964 that Seattle welcomed its first African American police officer to be promoted to the rank of sergeant. Walter Vernon Lawson earned that title and rapidly scaled the ranks of the Seattle Police Department. He became a lieutenant in July 1967 and then a captain in July 1969.

Bring in the Ladies!

Back in the day when Washington was first being settled, men grew tired of their own company—and a little lonely for members of the fairer sex. A wife was what most men wanted, but the few local women that were living there in 1864 were all married.

Along came Asa Mercer. He'd heard of the lack of marriageable women in the Seattle area from his brother, a local judge. Once he arrived and got a look for himself, he couldn't have agreed more. So he headed back east to Massachusetts. Although sources differ on the number of unmarried maidens accompanying Mercer out west to find themselves a husband, at least eight women were believed to have made the trip, and they arrived in Washington on May 16, 1864.

With one successful attempt under his belt, Mercer set out to find another batch of young, marriage-minded maidens. He set his sights high this time, hoping to convince another 1000 women to join him out west. While it's no surprise he didn't manage to talk that many women into joining him, 34 did make the second trip in May 1866. Among these eligible maidens, a Miss Annie E. Stephens captured Mercer's heart, and the two were married on July 15, 1866.

DID YOU  KNOW?

The women that Mercer brought west with him became known as the "Mercer Girls," and a television show based on the women—*Here Come the Brides*—debuted nearly 100 years later and was on the air from 1968 to 1970.

King of Bootleggers

Born on September 18, 1886, in Nebraska, Roy Olmstead began life in an ordinary way. With parents of good farming stock, he knew the meaning of hard work. By 1904, the young lad was working in the Moran Brothers Co. shipyard in Seattle, and just three years later, he joined the Seattle Police Department. By 1910, he had been promoted to sergeant and was joined by brothers Frank and Ralph on the force. His life seemed to be moving along quite nicely.

CHANGE IN THE AIR
But on November 1, 1914, life as he knew it began to change. Washingtonians voted to join 22 other states prohibiting the production and sale of alcoholic beverages. Olmstead continued his good work on the police force. He earned notoriety as the youngest lieutenant on the force in 1919. Although he wasn't a member of what was known as the "Dry Squad," Olmstead had been involved in raiding and arresting several bootleggers. And it wasn't long before it occurred to him that these "criminals" were caught only because of poor organization and stupid mistakes. He also noticed that even with their imperfect setups, the bootleggers were obviously making pretty good coin. So when even tougher legislation was enacted on January 1, 1920, Olmstead jumped on board the bootlegging bandwagon of the day.

LIFE ON THE DARK SIDE

Olmstead's attempt at being one of the "bad guys" wasn't as successful as his work as a police officer, and he, along with another police officer, nine bootleggers, six automobiles and nearly 100 cases of Canadian whiskey, were apprehended by Prohibition Bureau Agents in March 1920. Of course, he was dismissed from his position on the force and fined $500 after pleading guilty to charges of bootlegging in federal court. Ironically enough, this left Olmstead with nothing but time on his hands to expand his bootlegging efforts, and for another four years, he earned a pretty penny at the job. But this, too, would not last, and on November 26, 1924, he was arrested and subsequently tried, fined $8000 and sentenced to four years in the McNeil Island Federal Penitentiary.

A New Life

When he walked out of prison on May 12, 1931, it was as a changed man. He'd converted to the Christian Science faith and now believed liquor was a destructive force in society. Olmstead died on April 30, 1966. And though he spent his last 35 years dedicating himself to counseling, visiting jails and teaching the Bible, he is still known in Seattle as "King of the Puget Sound Bootleggers."

"Keep Clam"

In case you hadn't heard the saying before, "Keep Clam" is the company motto of Seattle icon Ivar Haglund. Born in that city in 1905, Haglund was not only a recognized media figure of his day, he also established a seafood restaurant called Ivar's Acres of Clams on Seattle's waterfront in 1946. That venture expanded to include three restaurants, nearly 30 fish bars throughout the Pacific Northwest and Ivar's own brand of clam chowder.

Haglund constantly created havoc and laughs with his antics wherever he went. In February 1947, when a tank car spilled tons of corn syrup all over the street on the waterfront, right outside his establishment, he quickly ordered himself up some pancakes and sat down in the street—spooning up syrup over his plate. The press arrived, and the photo "The Great Syrup Spill of 1947" hit the wires and was circulated around the world. Ivar had regular wacky television commercials for his restaurants and starred in many of them. One such TV advertisement starred Ivar playing his acoustic guitar and singing the song he penned, "Acres of Clams"—a song that showed up on his placemats and in his radio ads as well.

Haglund died in 1985, but the "Fourth of Jul-Ivar's" fireworks—a tradition Haglund began back in 1964—still light up the bay near Pier 54 every year.

 Ivar Hagland, in his typical wacky style, actually suggested that a postage stamp be made to honor the clam, instead of the planned USPS sardine stamp in 1960. In a letter he sent to a then–U.S. senator, he explained: "The sardine has been swimming around witlessly being gobbled up by the smarter fish ever since the Mesozoic Age...Clams keep their mouth shut...and never stick their necks out when the enemy is around."

Reshaping the Landscape

Back in Seattle's early days, one settler took the idea of shaping his community quite literally. In fact, Reginald H. Thomson seemed to believe a city should be founded on flat ground and began doing just that—leveling the natural landscape where the city was founded. In his capacity as city engineer, he is said to have "leveled hills, straightened and dredged waterways, reclaimed tide flats, built sewers, sidewalks, tunnels, and bridges and paved roads." In short, anything standing in the way of any of these tasks was simply bulldozed. In all, 25 miles of streets were regraded, displacing 16 million cubic yards of earth, which was then used to fill in the tidal flats on Seattle's south side.

A man of vision, Thomson is also credited with developing a water pipeline from the Cedar River Watershed 30 miles southeast of Seattle to secure a water source for the growing city. Water first flowed through those pipes on January 10, 1901. Thomson further harnessed the river's power to bring electricity to Seattle in 1905.

WARS AND CONFLICT

The Whitman Massacre

On November 29, 1847, 14 white settlers and missionaries were murdered by the Cayuse tribe and, for several weeks, 53 women and children were held captive and ransomed before being released. It was thought that the Cayuse believed the missionary Marcus Whitman to be an evil shaman who was using measles to murder their people. Unfortunately, there had been a measles outbreak, and while the white settlers were not falling ill, the Cayuse were dying. They mistakenly believed that Whitman's attempts to save them were efforts to curse them instead. An interpretive center marks the National Historic Site, where the mass grave of the massacre victims is located in Walla Walla.

The Cayuse War

In response to the Whitman Massacre, 500 militiamen led by fundamentalist clergyman Cornelius Gilliam and supported by the U.S. army marched into Cayuse territory. The Cayuse went into hiding in the Blue Mountains, and the military tried to track them, but it wasn't until 1850 that the Cayuse gave up five members to be tried for the murder of the Whitmans. The men were convicted and hanged on June 3, 1850. Unfortunately, this didn't end the fighting, which went on until the Cayuse surrendered in 1855. You can probably guess what happened next— the tribal people were placed on a reservation and most of their lands were taken. The next 40 years of relations were tense and often violent, all stemming from the initial Whitman conflict.

DID YOU  KNOW?

Seattle's Golden Gardens Park, commonly referred to as just "Golden Gardens," once housed military personnel. In fact, Washington was a common point of departure for many World War II soldiers.

Japanese Internment

While Washington State was and continues to be a place with a large Asian population, including the Japanese, when World War II broke out, the federal government decreed that all Japanese Americans would have to relocate their families to "camps" surrounded by barbed wire and guards. This move uprooted many established communities in the area and destroyed a number of successful businesses, most of which were unrecoverable once their owners were released.

NOTABLE EVENTS AND CONTRIBUTIONS

Washington Defines Its Boundaries

In 1863, the boundaries of the Idaho Territory were defined, and Washington's boundaries became those that currently exist.

Women Granted the Right to Vote

Washington became one of the first states in the union to approve women's suffrage in the 1910 election.

Prohibition Arrives

Prohibition passed into law in the election of 1915 and went into effect on January 1, 1916. Imagine the New Year's Eve of 1915!

First Woman Elected to Office

Belle Reeves was elected as Chelan County House member for the 1923–27 term and from 1931–37. She became the Secretary of State and was the first woman to hold a statewide elective office other than that of Superintendent of Public Instruction.

DID YOU KNOW?

In 1865, the University of Washington had a total of 15 students enrolled.

Father's Day Founder

Sonora Smart Dodd (1882–1978) was the originator of Father's Day, which began in Spokane in 1910. Not only is it an observed holiday in the U.S., but in many other nations as well.

Why Father's Day? In 1909, when Dodd was 27, she heard a Sunday sermon about Mother's Day and didn't understand why there wasn't such a day for fathers. As her father was a Civil War veteran and a widower, she felt he should have a day to be honored as well, so she began a campaign. She succeeded in convincing the Spokane Ministerial Association and the local YMCA to pass a resolution in support of Father's Day, and it was celebrated for the first time on June 19, 1910, in Spokane.

The idea spread, and other states began lobbying Congress for a national, annual Father's Day. In 1916, President Woodrow Wilson approved the notion, but it didn't really take off until President Calvin Coolidge made it a national event in 1924. In 1966, President Lyndon Johnson formally signed a presidential proclamation making the third Sunday of June Father's Day in the United States. Dodd was honored for her contribution at the Spokane World's Fair in 1974.

Hydroelectric Power Comes to Washington... via Washington (DC, that is)

Washington's rivers gave it a unique potential to generate hydroelectric power, something President Franklin D. Roosevelt had a great interest in exploiting. In fact, during his presidential campaign, he promised that, if elected, he would provide new jobs to the Northwest by building a dam. As this was during the Great Depression, the promise of jobs held great persuasive power. Under Roosevelt's directive, the government's Public Works Association funded the building of the Bonneville Dam on the Columbia River in 1937, followed by the Grand Coulee Dam in 1940.

Sure enough, jobs were brought to the area; furthermore, this act of Roosevelt's had a long-term impact on the future of development in the state. The existence of the dams meant that the state had the cheapest power in the country, and when World War II

came, Washington was the logical place to build aluminum production plants. Shipbuilders and aircraft manufacturers followed, which is how Boeing initially came to the state. Boeing has since become one of the largest employers to Washingtonians.

About the same time, the Hanford nuclear plant also located on the Columbia and was the site of clandestine military operations. Turns out that the plutonium used in the atomic bomb was manufactured at the site, and citizens living in the area in towns such as Richland became ill from the effects of radiation leaks.

DID YOU  KNOW?

FDR's decision to build a dam for cheap power in Washington was seen as folly by many, who called it the "Dam of Doubt" and "Roosevelt's White Elephant." Why? They didn't see how the country could possibly use all that electricity! Ironically, the cheaper power actually helped accelerate the growth of electrical use, and more generators were installed at the dam before it was even completed.

The Bonneville Dam produces over one million kilowatts of power. To put that in context, a 60-watt lightbulb uses, well, 60 watts of electricity. There are 1000 watts in a single kilowatt. In other words, that dam can light a lot of bulbs!

DID YOU KNOW?

An Olympia Dairy Queen was the first establishment in the world to have a soft-serve ice cream machine.

PLACE NAMES

Auburn

Auburn was originally named Slaughter in honor of Lieutenant W.A. Slaughter, who was killed by Natives nearby in 1855. In 1893, an objection to the name was filed, and the state legislature substituted Auburn for Slaughter. The name was taken from a line of poetry, "Sweet Auburn, loveliest village of the plain," from "The Deserted Village" by Oliver Goldsmith.

Ballard

The town is named for Captain William Rankin Ballard, who purchased several hundred acres of land there in 1882.

Bellevue

This decorative name was chosen by Oliver F. Franz when he surveyed and mapped the town in 1904. The name holds no special meaning.

Ellensburg

Named Ellen's Burgh after the wife of a settler, Mary Ellen Shoudy, postal officials later changed the name to Ellensburg.

Ephrata

Prior to the construction of the Grand Coulee Dam, irrigation was provided by using local springs, and this town's name reflects that. It was named for the Palestinian village of Ephrata, mentioned in the Old Testament as Ephratah, the predecessor to Bethlehem, which was irrigated by wells. Great Northern Railroad Company surveyors came up with that in 1892.

Everett

Everett Colby of New Jersey is this town's namesake. His father, Charles L. Colby, invested heavily in the area, after being enticed by settler Henry Hewitt. Hewitt heard that one of John D. Rockefeller's associates, Charles L. Colby, was looking for place to settle his American Steel Barge Company. Hewitt convinced Colby that the (modern-day Everett) peninsula with river and bay access was the perfect location. Colby formed a syndicate that included Rockefeller, Colby and Colgate Hoyt of the Great Northern Railroad. In the fall of 1890, the group formed the Everett Land Company and named Hewitt president. In the spring of 1891, land was cleared and a nail factory, barge works, paper mill and smelter were built, and a townsite was created. The name Everett was chosen as the town's name, after the son of Charles Colby.

Fremont

Once its own town (now part of Seattle), it was named by L.H. Griffith, who built a subdivision there. He named it after his hometown of Fremont, Nebraska.

The Seattle neighborhood of Fremont, which has christened itself the "Center of the Universe," is known for its out-there funkiness—and it has the statues to prove it! Fremont possesses the largest Lenin statue, weighing 7 tons, in the U.S., as well as the 18-foot-tall *Fremont Troll* under the Aurora Bridge and *Waiting for the Interurban*, with six figures cast in aluminum forever paying homage to the railway that used to connect Seattle with other local cities.

Magnolia
This town was named by Captain George Davidson of the U.S. Coast Survey in 1856. He confused the native madrona trees... with magnolias!

Madison Park
This neighborhood was named for Madison Avenue in Seattle's downtown, which in turn was named for President James Madison. The aboriginal name for the neighborhood was Xe-xt-l, which meant "where one chops." It turns out that Madison Park was the area that the Natives took wood from to build dugout canoes.

Mount Adams
This mountain was named in 1841 by the Wilkes expedition to honor President John Adams. The Native name for it was Pah-too, meaning "high, sloping mountain." Mount Adams has a central dome with four summits and supports eight major glaciers that supply nearby waterways.

Mount Baker

The name for this peak was provided by Captain George Vancouver in 1792, to honor Third Lieutenant Joseph Baker who was under his command and made the discovery.

DID YOU KNOW?

Mount Baker is the second most glaciated volcano in the Cascade Range, and it is home to an incredible amount of snow and ice. In fact, it's got more than all the other Cascade volcanoes combined, exclusive of Mount Rainier. In 1999, Mount Baker set the official world record for snowfall—1140 inches for the 1998–99 winter season.

Mount Constitution

This mountain in Moran State Park on Orcas Island was named
for the USS *Constitution* (aka "Old Ironsides"), made famous in
the War of 1812. The Natives, however, called this mountain
Sweh-lagh.

Mount Rainier

Captain George Vancouver named this peak to honor Rear
Admiral Peter Rainier, RN, Admiral of the Blue, in 1792.
Aboriginal names for the mountain included Tu-ah-ku, Puak-
coke, Ta-co-be, Ta-co-pe and Ta-ho-ma, meaning "snowy
mountain." Mount Rainier is 14,410 feet high and has long
been considered an icon of the Northwest.

DID YOU KNOW?

Mount Rainier is still an active volcano and is fully expected to
erupt at some time in the future. The last eruptions are said
to have occurred between 1820 and 1894, when 14 eruptions
were recorded. This peak is the highest point in the Cascade
mountain range and is the most glaciated mountain in the lower
48 states, encompassing 35 square miles of glacier pack.

Poulsbo

Poulsbo was 90 percent or more Scandinavian when it was
originally settled, with the bulk of its population hailing from
Norway. The town was named by resident Iver Brynildsen after
the town of Poulsbomoen in the Enning Valley, Halden, Norway.

Puyallup

This town takes its name from the Native name for the area,
Pough-allup, meaning "generous people," because tribes living
along the river there were reputed to be exceptionally generous.

Queen Anne Hill

This Seattle neighborhood was named by frontiersman Reverend Daniel Bagley when he noticed that many of the prosperous citizens who built houses there did so in the Queen Anne architectural style.

Redmond

This area on the east side of Lake Washington was named for Luke McRedmond, who founded the town and was its first postmaster.

Richmond Beach

This suburb of Seattle was named after a local landowner who hailed from Richmond, England.

Seattle

The city was named after the head of the Suquamps and allied tribes, Chief Sealth, whose name in English is "Seattle." It was given his name for two primary reasons: the chief was a tremendous help to the settlers in smoothing relationships between the Natives and the newcomers; and the chief was a friend to Doc Maynard, who suggested it. The Native name for the site of the city was Tzee-tzee-lal-itc, meaning "little place where one crosses over," which referred to a trail that began at the foot of Yesler Way and led to Lake Washington.

Snohomish

Snohomish is believed to be a variation of the Native word Sda-hob-bish, meaning "Tidewater People."

Snoqualmie

This town is named after a powerful tribe that lived there prior to the area being settled. The name given them by other tribes was, phonetically, Sdoh-kwahlb-bhuh, meaning "not of much account, but strong." Evidently this tribe ridiculed others and was not well liked.

Spokane

The name Spokane is thought to be from the aboriginal word Spehkunne, which means "Children of the Sun" or "Sun People." Legend says that when the Natives living at the foot of the Spokane Falls fished, they stood in a rainbow or halo of light that formed when the sun hit the misty waters splashed up by the falls. Another theory is that the town was named after Illum Spokane, a long-standing chief of the Middle Spokans tribe.

Stevens Pass

This town's namesake is John F. Stevens, the Great Railway engineer who built the first railway through the area in the early 1890s.

Tacoma

The name Tacoma was suggested by Philip Ritz, a Northern Pacific Railway official and was taken from Theodore Winthrop's book *The Canoe and the Saddle*.

DID YOU KNOW?

The *Pacific Tribune*, Tacoma's first newspaper, was first published on August 9, 1873, by Thomas Prosch.

Vancouver

This city is named to honor Captain George Vancouver, who explored the Columbia River area in 1792.

Walla Walla

The Native name Walla Walla translates into "place of many waters," which suggests the numerous tributaries of the Walla Walla River and the many other streams and springs that surround it.

Whidbey Island

The island was named in 1792 in honor of Joseph Whidbey, who proved that this piece of land was in fact an island when he explored Deception Pass in his ship the *Discovery*.

DID YOU KNOW?

Whidbey Island is the second largest island in the lower 48 states, with an area of 235 square miles.

Winthrop

This town was named by Congressman John. L. Wilson after Theodore Winthrop, the author of *The Canoe and the Saddle*.

Yakima

The aboriginal term *E-yak-kah-ma* or *Yah-ah-ka-ma* translates roughly to "black bear," with the plural ending "ma." The name has also been interpreted to mean "runaway," which fits a Native legend used to explain the city's name. Legend has it that a chief's daughter became pregnant out of wedlock and then either ran away or was banished to Yakima.

UNIQUE PLACES

Bickleton

The Whoop-N-Holler Museum is a good reason to take a trip to Bickleton, where you can spend the afternoon at Lawrence and Ada Ruth Whitmore's ranch. A large barn on the premises is full of old cars—Model T Fords, antique pickups, horse-drawn wagons, Studebakers—and is the largest such collection in the state. Early frontier memorabilia is displayed in the 1900 schoolhouse and throughout other buildings on the property.

You Never Know What a Can Might Lead to...
Bickleton has yet another claim to fame. It has taken on responsibility for the endangered bluebird and is known as the "Bluebird Capital of the World."

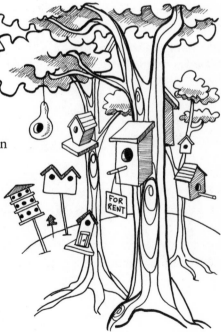

How did this title come to be? According to legend, Jess and Elva Brinkerhoff stopped in the town for a picnic in the 1950s, put a can in a tree for some birds and somehow or other it became a popular thing for residents to do. There are now thousands of birdhouses built expressly for the local bluebirds.

Centralia

Centralia citizens got crafty during Seattle's 1962 World's Fair and decided to divert some of the tourists headed to the city to their town instead. To do so, then built a 150-foot-high Space Needle replica (Seattle's Space Needle was a major 1962 World's Fair attraction) that included its own "astronaut," played by 18-year-old Loren Wolff. Loren would chat with tourists on the phone from his perch at the top of Centralia's replica "Needle" as they called from a phone at the base.

Poulsbo

Poulsbo, founded by Norwegian settlers in the 1880s, is located at the head of Liberty Bay in Puget Sound, an area that is supposedly similar in topography to the fjords of Norway. Festivals celebrating the founders' Scandinavian heritage continue today and include the Viking Fest in May, the Skandia Midsommarfest, which celebrates the summer solstice, in June and a Yule Fest in December that includes a traditional Yule log lighting and the arrival of Father Christmas.

Ephrata

This town east of the mountains features the Pioneer Village and Museum. The village has 30 life-size buildings, including a saloon, dress shop, barbershop, watch repair shop, Catholic church, jail, printing office, blacksmith and more. The buildings are a combination of original structures and reproductions.

Hoquiam

A mansion built in the late 1800s by lumber tycoon Robert Lytle, known as the "castle," is a popular tourist attraction. It boasts 20 rooms full of Victorian furnishings, complete with a re-created saloon that helps provide a sense of the time period.

Dayton: Home to the "Other" Weinhard Beer Family

Dayton has both the oldest train depot in the state, built in 1881, and the oldest working county courthouse, constructed in 1887. The area was intially visited and written about by Lewis and Clark on their famous expedition, and the townsite was settled in the mid-1800s. There are 117 buildings built between 1880 and 1910 that are listed on the National Register of Historic Places, and Dayton has three National Historic Districts for visitors to tour. In 1882, the city was the third largest in the Washington Territory behind Seattle and Walla Walla. Jacob Weinhard (nephew of Henry, the brewmaster, with whom he apprenticed in Portland) moved to the town with the intention of starting his own brewery and following in his uncle Henry's footsteps. By 1904, he had built a small empire that included a brewery, malt house, saloon, lodge hall and theater. The Weinhard Hotel is still open for business in Dayton, and while it has modern conveniences such as Internet connections, it maintains its Victorian charm. Believe it or not, they even rent Surrey bikes for two that guests can ride to tour the town.

Edmonds: Living Here Increases "Famous Potential"

Edmonds sits on Puget Sound and has been home to an unusual number of talented Washingtonians, including Ken Jennings, who holds the record for the longest winning streak on the game show *Jeopardy!*; Rick Steves, an internationally known travel writer and travel show host; Rosalyn Sumners, the Olympic figure-skating medalist; actor Steven Bailey; and actress Anna Faris. What's their secret sauce?

Goldendale: A Good Place to Watch the Stars

Goldendale Observatory State Park, which sits on a 2100-foot-high hill near Goldendale, houses the largest public telescopes in the United States.

In 1980, the observatory was purchased by the state after having been operated by the Goldendale Observatory Corporation since 1973. The observatory dome has a diameter of 20 feet, and its largest telescope is 24 inches in diameter, making it one of the world's most powerful public scopes.

Lynden: Little Deutschland

The town of Lynden was founded in 1891 and experienced a large influx of Dutch immigrants in the early to mid-1900s. Dutch heritage is celebrated in the town's architecture and businesses. There is a Dutch bakery, several restaurants and many antique stores. Even the local supermarkets have Dutch specialty food sections! The town also has the Lynden Pioneer Museum, housing a unique collection of frontier artifacts, including 40 antique buggies, wagons and carts.

Republic: Forget T-shirts and Bring Home Your Own Fossils!

Fifty million years ago, this tiny town in Ferry County was under a lake, which filled in over time and is now a rich fossil bed. Visitors to the Stonerose Interpretive Center may purchase a ticket and dig for fossils. While all finds must be shown to the curator, each person is allowed to take home three fossils a day. Should someone dig up something scientifically significant, however, the museum reserves the right to keep it.

Roslyn: Home to Television's Homage to Eccentrics, *Northern Exposure*

Roslyn was the actual town where this popular 1990s show depicting the fictitious town of Cicely, Alaska, was filmed. Key show characters included the town doctor, Joel Fleischman (played by Rob Morrow), bush pilot Maggie O'Connell (played by Janine Turner), former astronaut and town founder Maurice Minnifield (played by Barry Corbin) and quirky deejay Chris Stevens (played by John Corbett). The town still has the Brick (the bar that was the inspiration for Holling's Tavern), and the Roslyn Café still serves up a nice country meal just like Roslyn's Café on the show. But that's not all that makes Roslyn unique! The Brick tavern claims to be the oldest bar in Washington, and what's more, Roslyn is reputed to be the site of an 1892 bank robbery by the infamous duo of Butch Cassidy and the Sundance Kid.

Omak

Omak is home to the annual Omak Stampede and its famous Suicide Race, which the town touts as the "most dangerous race in the world."

The second weekend in August, riders on horseback stampede down 210-foot-long, 60-degree slope covered with wet sand in the full darkness of night. The horses are raced at full gallop 120 yards towards the drop-off and are near-blind on their descent.

Most human and horse injuries and deaths happen in this beginning stretch of the race. Those that make it past the first stage go from the slope into the Okanogan River, where they swim 50 yards (half a football field). If they cross the river successfully, the finish line is at the top of a steep grade. Those who

pass this first race continue through a series of four more races (based on survival, of course—many deaths, particularly of the horses, occur during these races). The winner gets a pot of about $15,000, plus two hand-tooled leather saddles. Many animal rights organizations have been trying to stop the race for years. The Humane Society of the United States and the Progressive Animal Welfare Society (PAWS) are just two of the groups that have spoken out against the event.

Stehekin: Elizabeth Taylor Once Stayed Here

The movie *Courage of Lassie* starring Elizabeth Taylor was filmed in Stehekin in 1944. The town also maintains the one-room schoolhouse built in 1921, which was used to educate the town's children until 1989, when a new school was constructed.

Tumwater: Historic Crosby House

Pioneer Nathaniel Crosby III built a house in Tumwater in 1858, and he and his wife went on to become the proud grandparents of singer Bing Crosby. The house is one of the oldest wood-framed houses in the state, and if you're interested, there are free tours two days a week. Tumwater's main claim to fame, though, is as "Washington's First Community." Founded in 1845, it was the first American township north of the Columbia River.

Winthrop: Home on the Range

The town of Winthrop was first settled in 1891 by men following the lure of gold to the area—a town that truly embodied the "American West." A man named Owen Wister honeymooned there and was so inspired that he wrote America's first western novel, *The Virginian*. The town did a full western restoration in 1972, when State Highway 20 was built, as a way to encourage visitors to share its history. Architect and designer Robert Jorgenson of Leavenworth worked hard to make the restoration as authentic as possible. The task was made easier because a good number of original false-front buildings were still intact.

Winlock: World's Largest Egg

The world's largest egg is reputed to be in Winlock, weighing in at 1200 pounds and measuring 12 feet long. Imagine the omelet this faux baby could make were it for real! Reclining on a pedestal on a 10-foot-high steel pole on a wide highway median running through the center of town, it screams out "World's Largest Egg, Winlock" from the sign on which it rests. There is an Egg Day Festival every year during the third week of June.

Fairfield

Fairfield is home to Ye Galleon Press, founded by Glen Adams (1911–93), who also served as mayor of Fairfield. Ye Galleon was the oldest active independent publishing house in the Pacific Northwest until Adams' death and prodcued 727 books covering a host of subjects about the Pacific Northwest and other rare U.S. history. According to Nancy Compau, director of the Northwest Room of the Spokane Public Library, one of the most valuable books that Ye Galleon published was Joseph Franklin's *All Through the Night: The History of Spokane Black Americans, 1860–1940*. "It was self-published, and it has inaccuracies," Compau stated. "On the other hand, it's about all that we have." Compau went on to note that Adams' "contribution to history was invaluable...even I can afford to buy some things that I never would be able to if he hadn't reprinted them."

Walla Walla

Famed for its Walla Walla sweet onions, the town holds a Sweet Onion Festival every year. As it turns out, though, the onions aren't actually from the state. In fact, they're not from the U.S. at all. Rather, seeds were brought to Washington in the late 1800s by a French soldier named Peter Pier, who discovered the onion on the island of Corsica off the west coast of Italy. Local Italians loved the flavor and its winter hardiness and shared the seeds widely, creating something of a phenomenon that continues to this day.

DID YOU KNOW?

Regular onions have high levels of sulfur compounds, which in turn contain pyruvic acid. Chopping onions releases the acid, causing tears. Real sweet onions are grown in soil with low amounts of sulfur and thus have low pyruvic acid levels. Sweet onions don't cause tearing.

SMALL TOWN ODDITIES

Bobo: The Gorilla in Our Midst

A small-town star, the newborn Bobo was brought from French
Equatorial Africa to America by a hunter and was purchased by
Bill Lowman in Columbus, Ohio, in 1951. Lowman brought
the gorilla home to Anacortes, where three generations of the
Lowman family resided—and there Bobo lived happily for
about two and a half years, especially bonding with his
"Grandma," Lowman's mother. Bobo was dressed in children's
clothing and ate at the table, and he was considered a member
of the family until he got too big for the house. Evidently, he
was breaking dishes too often. At this point, the family reluc-
tantly gave him to the Woodland Park Zoo, where he was a

main attraction until his death in 1968. The family continued visit him over the years—they brought a cake to him on his fifth birthday, an event that brought media attention. Bobo recognized them and was interested in socializing for several years after he was moved. Sadly, after his death, Bobo was stuffed (though out of love!) and is still on display at Seattle's Museum of History and Industry.

Bavaria...er, Leavenworth, I mean...

A small community in the mountains of eastern Washington, Leavenworth hit hard times in the 1960s and was facing the real possibility of becoming a ghost town. Instead, residents got creative and decided to rebuild the town, but this time with a marketing plan. They set off to recreate a small village in Bavaria, Germany. So meticulous were they with their planning that even the local McDonalds adheres to the Bavarian style. The town's annual Christmas tree lighting celebration draws thousands of tourists, as does its Germanic architecture and shops during the rest of the year. Is it based on reality? Well, no. But it certainly has worked, and the town has continued to thrive. To be fair, it has also worked hard to be authentic, and in so doing has gone from an almost zero percent German population to 30 percent!

Mima Mounds

A prairie full of bumpy earth, which looks like moguls on a ski slope, covers 445 acres of land in Littlerock. The mounds once covered 30,000 acres before development took over the unpreserved land. What exactly the mounds are and how they got there is still something of a mystery. Many scientists have written papers promoting various hypotheses, but a consensus has yet to be reached. Some say they are the work of pocket gophers that no longer inhabit the area. Others promote the notion that temperature changes after the last ice age caused the earth to buckle and form the mounds.

DISASTROUS EVENTS

The Nez Perce Showdown

Chief Joseph (1840–1904), aka Hin-mah-too-yah-lat-kekh, meaning "Thunder Traveling to Loftier Mountain Heights," fought the U.S. government's desire to put his tribe onto reservations. Chief Joseph and his tribe had a history of good relationships with the early settlers. In fact, Joseph spent many of his growing-up years at a Christian mission. The conflict was regarding a new treaty that the U.S. said overruled an 1855 treaty that provided for much more land. The Nez Perce said they had never agreed to a new treaty, and the war was on. The conflict lasted four months, and the Nez Perce traveled over 1000 miles, eluding the U.S. military and trying to get to Canada. Five major battles occurred in 1877, with the last happening at Bear Paw, just 40 miles south of the Canadian border. Approximately 200 Nez Perce escaped, but about 425 surrendered and were forced onto a reservation. Chief Joseph continued to appeal to the federal government in Washington, DC, but all attempts failed. Joseph died on a reservation in 1904, apparently of a "broken heart."

When Chief Joseph surrendered to the U.S. military after failing to reach the Canadian border, he said: "From where the sun now stands, I will fight no more forever."

The Great Seattle Fire

On June 6, 1889, a great blaze broke out in Seattle, burning 29 city blocks and utterly annihilating the majority of the business district. Amazingly, not a single person was killed. The city had to rebuild and essentially did so on top of the damaged streets. Today, one can tour the original streets via the Underground Seattle tour.

The Luna Park Blaze

New York Alki (West Seattle's original name) was once an amusement park modeled after Coney Island in New York. It was stocked with rides and games, including a figure-eight roller coaster, a merry-go-round, Chute-the-Chutes, a water slide, the Cave of Mystery, the Canal of Venice, the Original Human Ostrich, the Joy Wheel and the Infant Electrobator! It also boasted the best-stocked bar on Elliot Bay. The park was a hit, and as the streetcar had a line running from Seattle directly to Alki, it didn't want for business. Unfortunately, the park was destroyed in a fire in 1913, only six years after it had opened.

"Galloping Gertie," aka the Tacoma Narrows Bridge

On November 7, 1940, the third largest suspension bridge in the world fell apart, dropping a 600-square-foot section 195 feet into Puget Sound below. Amazingly, the only casualty was a dog named Tubby that had been stuck in an abandoned car on the bridge deck. The Washington Department of Transportation refers to the collapse as "the most spectacular failure in bridge engineering history."

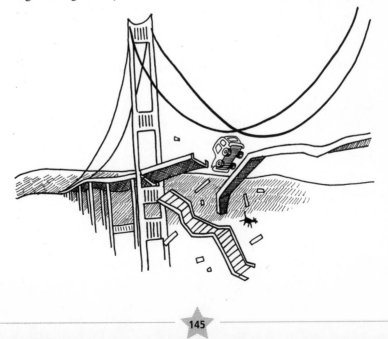

The mile-long bridge collapsed because of wind vibrations. It was designed by Washington State engineer Clark Eldridge and altered by designer Leon Moisseiff, famed for his design of San Francisco's Golden Gate Bridge.

The original Narrows bridge was the first suspension bridge to employ plate girders (or deep I-beams) to support the roadbed. With earlier suspension bridge designs, wind would pass through the truss, but in the Narrows design, the wind was forced above and below the structure. Thus, the bridge swayed and buckled in the wind because the moving air created longitudinal resonance along the bridge's length, both up and down and side to side, earning it the nickname "Galloping Gertie." The bridge collapsed when the wind produced a twisting mode in the bridge—the structure literally twisted itself to pieces.

After the original bridge fell, it was rebuilt with open trusses, stiffening struts and openings in the roadway that allowed wind to pass through, alleviating the longitudinal resonance issue. The new bridge was completed on October 14, 1950, and was 5979 feet long—40 feet longer than the original. It is today considered the fifth longest suspension bridge in the United States and is affectionately called "Sturdy Gertie."

DID YOU KNOW?

The Canadian band the Tragically Hip reference Gertie in their 2004 song "Vaccination Scar": "It went down like a bad card table, like the Tacoma Narrows Bridge."

LIFE IN WASHINGTON

The Great Outdoors

One thing tourists tend to notice when they visit Washington is that they are often overdressed—for everything. Including, say, the grocery store. Residents of the state love to be comfortable and spend time in the outdoors in every season.

Outdoor activities are huge—and that doesn't just mean sports-related activities. In fact, Washington is a state full of *watchers* as well. Specifically, wildlife watching. In 2001, 47 percent of Washington's residents participated in wildlife watching, whereas only 30 percent did nationally.

Sixteen percent of residents fished and five percent hunted. Birdwatching is a primary wildlife viewing activity, and state

residents have the fourth-highest participation rate in the country—36 percent of Washingtonians look for birds regularly.

While you might think all this "watching" doesn't get the state very far, the truth is that it can result in huge economic outputs derived from money spent on such things as trips and equipment; in 2001, that output was $1.78 billion—the eighth highest in the nation.

Watching, of course, isn't the only thing that residents excel at. Many of them actively participate in nature by hiking, rock climbing, biking, skiing...the list goes on.

DID YOU KNOW?

Washington even has some outdoor record-breakers on hand—long-time resident Jim Whittaker was the first American to scale Mount Everest successfully in 1963, and he still hikes Mount Rainier at the age of 77!

Alternative Lifestyles

The Seattle metropolitan area is second only to San Francisco in terms of male same-sex unmarried-partner household prevalence in metropolitan statistical areas (MSAs). Seattle also has the highest number of female same-sex unmarried-partner households—actually exactly the same percentage as for gay males—0.5 percent of metro area couples.

DRUGS, BOOZE AND ALL THINGS NAUGHTY

Drug-Smuggling Tunnel

In 2005, a group of Canadian drug smugglers decided to build a tunnel between a greenhouse in Langley, British Columbia, and the basement of a house in Lynden, Washington. The tunnel ran 360 feet underneath the U.S.-Canada border. Were it not for a neighbor noticing that a lot of stuff was entering the greenhouse and nothing but dirt was coming out, marijuana might still be crossing the border underground. Customs officers set up surveillance devices, and the smuggling crew was arrested soon after the tunnels were completed and the smuggling began.

Hempfest

This annual event brings music and vendors together with activists to discuss marijuana and hemp policy reform and ongoing related events nationwide. It started in 1991 as the "Washington Hemp Expo" in Volunteer Park in Seattle but has since expanded into Myrtle Edwards Park on the downtown Seattle waterfront.

The year 2005 was a landmark for the festival, as many noteworthy speakers came to speak to the crowds, including Rob Kampia from the Marijuana Policy Project, Jack Cole of Law Enforcement Against Prohibition, Stephen Gaskin from the Farm Commune and medical patient Angel Raich.

Wine Country

Washington has gone from a state with 10 wineries 30 years ago to one with more than 400 today. The growth has been astounding, and what's more, the wines are good. Many are so good, in fact, that they are the bestselling wines of their kind in the nation, outselling even Californian wines.

The climate of eastern Washington, in particular, is considered to be ideal for growing grapes—arid and dry in the summer and cold in the winter—thus building "character" into the product. The soil ("terroir") of Walla Walla excites many wine experts. Coincidentally, Walla Walla is on the 46th parallel, which means that its latitude is roughly the same as that of Burgundy, France, which is, of course, known for its fine wines.

WORK

Well Paid

Washington comes out in the top 10 for national wages in 18 of 22 categories measured. It is third in the nation for pay in "protective services" and fourth in a full six other categories, including arts, design, entertainment, sports and media, management, and architecture and engineering.

A Good Report Card

The twice-annual Development Report Card published by the nonprofit Corporation for Enterprise Development (CFED) ranks each state's best practices, and in 2006, Washington was sitting pretty.

The state ranked:

☞ first for short-term employment growth;

☞ second for creation of new companies;

☞ third for venture capital investments;

☞ fourth for private R and D;

☞ and fifth for low-cost energy.

Not too shabby!

Jobs and Unemployment

The year 2005 was a good one for Washington; unemployment actually decreased from the previous year—something that hasn't happened since 2001!

For 2005, state unemployment stood at 5.6 percent, compared to 6.2 percent in 2004. The Seattle metro area had the largest number of people employed, with only 4.7 percent lacking a job, whereas the Yakima metro area (one of Washington's great wine regions) had the highest level of unemployed, at 7.7 percent for 2005.

What's most interesting is the industry that made up the bulk of job growth. One might be inclined to look towards aerospace, for instance, or technology...but, in fact, construction was responsible for 20 percent of the employment growth percentage.

To clarify, it's important to understand that while construction and extraction occupations (primarily construction) and healthcare support occupations are expected to continue with substantial growth in their employment shares in the short term (through 2007), the long view has growth rates in construction and extraction employment declining. The fastest-growing occupations are expected to remain in the areas of computers and mathematics, along with personal care and service. Washington is still the number one technology employer; in 2003, 10 percent of all jobs in the state were in high-tech industries.

Washington's Top Employers

The top 10 employers in Washington State for 2005, ranked by the number of employees working in the state (many of these companies have employees in other states), were as follows:

Rank	Employer	City	Number of Employees
1	Cingular Wireless	Redmond	31,000
2	University of Washington	Seattle	27,000
3	Seattle-Tacoma International Airport	Seatac	21,000
4	Microsoft	Redmond	20,000
5	Boeing	Auburn	10,000
6	Boeing	Kent	10,000
7	University of Washington—Ob/Gyn	Seattle	6000
8	Washington State University	Pullman	5770
9	BBSI	Moses Lake	5000
10	South Seattle Community College	Seattle	5000

Source: InfoUSA

DID YOU KNOW?

Boeing, founded in Seattle, is the largest aircraft manufacturer (by revenue) and the second largest defense contractor in the world. Boeing is also the largest exporter in America.

The Working Class

The years before World War I were full of strife for working-class folks who pitted themselves against businessmen. The Industrial Workers of the World (also called the IWW or the "Wobblies") had battles with business owners, both politically and physically. In fact, several deaths resulted from a confrontation between a boatload of Seattle Wobblies and law enforcement officers and citizens at the port of Everett, where they were attempting to disembark. This event, known as the Everett Massacre, resulted in new criminal laws being legislated in the 1917 session.

The Seattle area also had many citizens hailing from Scandinavia, where cooperative enterprises and government ownership were de rigueur. These immigrants tended to have a different perspective on political decisions, making for a unique tapestry of viewpoints.

That same sort of tapestry still exists today, and Washington notoriously has every side represented. The state trends towards a more liberal viewpoint, but it has seesawed over time.

DID YOU KNOW?

The term "skid row" originated in Seattle from the term "skid road." As the gold rush took off, the population of the city boomed, and logs were rolled down Skid Road (Yesler Way) to the busy port into the part of town that today is Pioneer Square. A 1937 magazine article incorrectly wrote "skid row" instead of "skid road," and the term was coined.

TRANSPORTATION

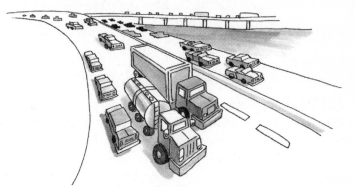

Major Highways

☛ State Route 14 (SR 14) is also known as the Lewis and Clark Highway. About 150 miles of the 200-mile-long roadway follow the Columbia River, providing an interesting scenic drive with ample roadside turnoffs to view the Columbia River Gorge and other areas. It is one of 44 state highways. Seven interstate highways and seven United States highways make their way through Washington.

☛ Interstate 90 (I-90) begins in Seattle and continues east, covering its first 297 miles through Washington State. Only New York (385 miles), Montana (552 miles), and South Dakota (412 miles) boast control of a larger portion of the nationwide highway. At 3100 miles in length, the I-90 is considered the longest highway in the world.

Road Travel in Washington

There are 39,832 miles of county roads, 16,261 miles of city streets, 16,078 miles of other state roads, 7251 miles of federal roads, 2765 miles of principal arterials, 1852 miles of minor arterials, 1665 miles of collectors and 764 miles of Interstate, making a grand total of 86,468 miles of roadways in the state.

Air Travel

In 2004, the Seattle-Tacoma International Airport serviced 28,804,554 passengers. Of those, 13,214,819 were domestic passengers traveling into Washington and 13,153,619 were leaving the state. The remaining 2,436,116 were international passengers, 1,224,493 were coming into the country and 1,210,623 were leaving.

DID YOU KNOW?

Interstate 90 traverses mountains and 13 states, and its tentacles reach many major cities, including Chicago, Toledo, Cleveland, Buffalo, Albany and Boston.

Traffic Trouble

Washington can be divided into two parts—east and west. In each of the two halves, only two cities have much traffic— Seattle on the west side of the mountains and Spokane on the east. Both cities have had ever-increasing traffic congestion problems for many years, according to the nationwide research performed annually by the Texas Transportation Institute.

The state has been busy attempting to solve transportation woes, coming up with plan after plan—most of which are rejected by voters or rethought at the last minute. One of the complicating factors is that the bulk of the traffic problem is relegated to the Seattle metropolitan area, and citizens on the east side of the state often don't pass legislation that would require them to supply part of the funding for the solution. One can certainly understand why, but it does lead to something of a conundrum for the "powers that be."

The Seattle Situation

The Seattle area is particularly challenged by traffic because of its unique geography. As the population increases, the existing roads end up grid-locked, and there aren't any ready expansion options.

An attempt was made to enlarge the small monorail system built for the 1962 World's Fair, but the project was canceled. In the meantime, railway lines are being built but won't be completed for many years, and then, too, they will only address certain areas. There is currently no solution on the table for one of the worst areas of congestion—from Seattle to the east side of Lake Washington, where companies such as Microsoft and Nintendo have their offices. Likewise, areas such as Ballard and West Seattle, both full of young families that commute into the city, don't have anything but the bus lines, which are limited and travel the same roadways already congested with automobiles.

The Olden Days

Interestingly, historical Seattle had infrastructure that would have helped traffic today had it been maintained. For example, by 1912, there was a private interurban train line connecting Tacoma, Seattle and Everett—pieces of which are now walking paths called the "Interurban" (many people don't know where the name comes from, but it's because the rail line used to pass through the areas). Furthermore, a streetcar line, whose first streetcars were pulled by horses but were later replaced by electric trolleys, began service in the area in 1884. A streetcar line ran from West Seattle to downtown and likewise from Ballard. Lake Washington even had a private ferry system running from Seattle to Kirkland!

Modern Mayhem

So...what the heck happened? How could the city go from having mass transportation infrastructure in the form of an intercity rail system, an electric trolley system and ferries connecting across Lake Washington to being one of the worst-congested traffic areas in the country? Well, the future could not be known, and it was thought that the automobile and individual travel along large roadways was where the nation was headed. Highway 99 was built. The city "modernized" by replacing streetcars with buses, and streetcar lines were ripped up in 1941. The Seattle-Tacoma Interurban Railway that began in 1902 and connected Tacoma, Renton, Seattle, Shoreline and other cities had gone bankrupt by 1927 thanks to the popularity of the automobile. The private ferry service that traveled from Seattle to Kirkland for 70 years made its last run in 1950, replaced by the SR-520 floating bridge and the popular belief that highways were the future of transportation.

What does the future hold for Washington in terms of mass transit? As of now, the state is slowly beginning to build an inter-city rail system on one side of the mountains, but beyond that, it's hard to say.

DID YOU KNOW?

People 65 years of age and older will soon account for a much larger share of Washington's population, increasing from 11 percent in 2000 to a predicted 20 percent in 2030. The percentages of older age groups in the workforce have been increasing steadily as far back as 1995 and will continue to do so into the foreseeable future.

ENTREPRENEURS AND THEIR COMPANIES

Boeing

William Edward Boeing (1881–1956) founded the Pacific Aero Products Company in Seattle in 1916, which became the Boeing Airplane Company in 1917. In 1961, the name was changed to the Boeing Company as they branched out beyond mere airplanes. William also founded Boeing Air Transport, which later morphed into United Airlines.

Boeing is the largest aircraft manufacturer in the world, specializing in jetliners and military aircraft. In 2006, it employed about 154,000 thousand people worldwide. While the company was based in Washington State for the majority of its existence, the corporate headquarters moved to Chicago, Illinois, on September 4, 2001, directly impacting about 1000 jobs at the time. Many arms of the company remain based in Washington, including: commercial airplanes, Boeing Capital Corp., air traffic management, Connexion by Boeing, military aircraft and missile systems, space and communications, and Phantom Works. At the time of the move, the company employed 78,400 people in the Seattle area and 198,900 people worldwide.

Nordstrom

John W. Nordstrom (1871–1963) was the co-founder of the Nordstrom department store chain. He was born in Luleå, Sweden, and came to the United States when he was 16, first settling in California and then moving north to Seattle. He was headed for the Klondike Gold Rush in Alaska, where he worked hard and made $13,000. While mining gold, he met a shoe-maker named Carl Wallin, and Nordstrom and Wallin settled back in Seattle in 1901, they opened a shoe store together called Wallin & Nordstrom at Fourth Avenue and Pike Street. Thus the retail empire began.

By 1923, Nordstrom and Wallin had opened a second shoe store. Not long after (in 1928) Nordstrom retired, selling his stake to his sons Everett and Elmer—who went on to purchase Wallin's shares. John Nordstrom's third son, Lloyd, joined the company as a part owner in 1933. By 1960, there were eight Nordstrom shoe stores in Washington and Oregon, and the original Seattle store became the largest such store in the United States. They had expanded into clothing by 1963, and members of the third generation Nordstrom family took over and con-tinue to oversee what is now Nordstrom, Inc.

Nordstrom is, of course, known for fabulous shoes and terrific customer service. People will often choose to pay a bit more for merchandise at Nordstrom because they know if there is any problem, the company will take care of it with no questions asked. Nordstrom is considered a leading fashion specialty retailer and employed approximately 52,000 full- or part-time workers in 2005. The company has stores in almost every major American city, totaling 156 stores in 27 states. The exception is Boston and Manhattan, though Nordstrom intends to build four stores in Boston beginning in 2007, with the first store currently planned for the Natick Mall.

DID YOU KNOW?

Nintendo's main corporate headquarters are located in Japan, but their Western Hemisphere headquarters are in Redmond, within spitting distance of one of its largest competitors—Microsoft. The two game console creators (Nintendo with its GameCube and the newly released Wii and Microsoft with its XBox) battle over who gets the number two spot, behind the gaming console leader Sony, who produces the PlayStation. Nintendo's Game Boy, however, is still the leading handheld gaming device in the world.

Microsoft

Bill Gates (b. 1955) was born and raised in the Seattle area and is the wealthiest man in the world (*Forbes* 2006), and he got there by founding the Microsoft Corporation in Albuquerque, New Mexico, in 1975 with his friend Paul Allen. In 1979, the company moved back to the Seattle area and headquartered in Redmond. Bill Gates is also known for being the world's greatest philanthropist, which came about with his creation of the Gates Foundation—an endeavor he plans on dedicating himself to full time when he retires from Microsoft in 2008. Paul Allen (b. 1953) was born in Seattle and is the sixth richest man in the world (*Forbes* 2006), largely because he co-founded Microsoft with childhood friend Bill Gates. Allen left Microsoft in 1983 but still resides in the

Seattle area, where he runs Vulcan, Inc. among many other endeavors, including two professional sport teams: the Seattle Seahawks (NFL) and the Portland Trail Blazers (NBA). Allen also has a passion for music, science-fiction and space. He has created the Experience Music Project (EMP) Museum in Seattle, the Science-Fiction Museum in Seattle and has sponsored the development of SpaceShipOne, the first privately developed spacecraft to attain suborbital space.

Microsoft celebrated its 30th anniversary in 2006, having grown from a private company founded by childhood friends to a global heavyweight employing 71,000 people on a full-time basis—44,000 in the United States and 27,000 internationally. Microsoft is the number one software company in the world, with computer software for desktops being its primary business. In addition, Microsoft also provides a variety of business solutions and consumer-oriented entertainment software, including the gaming platform XBox.

DID YOU KNOW?

Bill Gates and Paul Allen went to high school together at Lakeside School in Seattle and became friends, bonding over their shared love of computers. They were known to completely monopolize (foreshadowing, perhaps?) the school's single minicomputer system. Dissatisfied with the power of the minicomputer, the boys decided to go to the University of Washington and sneak into their computer lab. When they got caught (go figure), they negotiated use of the computers in exchange for providing computer help to students in the lab.

It was Allen who convinced Gates to drop out of Harvard to start Microsoft, after having dropped out of Washington State University himself after two years. Essentially, then, two of the richest men in the world don't have the college degrees. Perhaps degrees are overrated?

OTHER INDUSTRIES

Economic Diversity

Washington State counts many industries and their company leaders as residents. Boeing, the aerospace manufacturer, holds the title as America's leading exporter and manufactures many of its planes in the state. The world's number one software maker, Microsoft, is also headquartered here, and one of the country's most successful Internet businesses, Amazon.com, hails from the area. Washington, in fact, was home to nine Fortune 500 and 15 Fortune 1000 companies in 2006. In fact, the top five companies represent unique, distinct industries: specialty retailers, computer software, forest and paper products, savings institutions and motor vehicles and parts.

Rank	Company	Revenues ($ millions)	City
1	Costco Wholesale	52,935.2	Issaquah
2	Microsoft	39,788.0	Redmond
3	Weyerhaeuser	23,000.0	Federal Way
4	Washington Mutual	21,326.0	Seattle
5	Paccar	14,057.4	Bellevue
6	Amazon.com	8,490.0	Seattle
7	Nordstrom	7,722.9	Seattle
8	Starbucks	6,369.3	Seattle
9	Safeco	6,351.1	Seattle
10	Expeditors Intl. of Washington	3,901.8	Seattle
11	Alaska Air	2,975.3	Seattle
12	Puget Energy	2,966.5	Bellevue
13	Nextel Partners	1,801.7	Kirkland
14	Plum Creek Timber	1,576.0	Seattle
15	Potlatch	1,496.1	Spokane

World Class Ports

Washington's ports are also key to its industrial success. The state ranks number one in exports per capita, and overall, it is the fourth largest exporter in the nation. In fact, Seattle's container port is the fastest growing in the country, producing 18 percent year-over-year growth in 2005.

DID YOU  **KNOW?**

Washington produces more than half the apples grown in the United States. And if you love red raspberries, Washington's 2004 crop production was number one in the U.S., producing 90 percent of the country's red raspberries that year.

COST OF LIVING

A Dollar Earned

If you want to make a go of it, Washington is a good place to set down roots. Compared with the rest of the country, the state leads the pack when it comes to minimum wage rates, at $7.63 per hour. Twenty-three states mirror the federal minimum wage of $5.15 per hour. Kansas reports the lowest minimum wage, at $2.65 per hour, while Alabama, Arizona, Louisiana, Mississippi, South Carolina and Tennessee have no minimum wage.

The Tax Man

According to the Tax Foundation, spend your money in Washington and expect to pay another 6.5 percent in sales tax. Next to Tennessee, Rhode Island and Mississippi, which all have a seven percent sales tax, Washington charges the second highest sales tax along with Minnesota and Nevada.

On an up note, Washington is one of only seven states without personal income tax.

People in Poverty

Based on a three-year average spanning 2002 to 2004, Washington is about the middle of the pack when compared to other states, with 11.7 percent of their population living in poverty. Mississippi, Arkansas and New Mexico lead the states in poverty rates with 17.7, 17.6 and 17.5 percent respectively. Folks in New Hampshire appear to have the upper hand in this category, with only 5.7 percent of their population living at or below the poverty line. According to the U.S. Census Bureau, a family of four earning $19,307 or less in 2004 was considered to be living below the poverty threshold.

A Man's Castle

In 2005, about 67 percent of Washington families owned their own home, which falls just under the overall American average of 68.9 percent. West Virginia boasts the highest number of family-owned homes at 81.3 percent. New York State has the lowest percentage of family-owned homes at 55.9 percent.

How Big is Your Family?
In 2004, households in Washington could be broken down as follows:

- ☞ 112,000 total households;

- ☞ 26.4 percent were single-person households;

- ☞ 33.4 percent of households were comprised of two people;

- ☞ 16.0 percent were three-person households;

- ☞ 14.3 percent were four-person households;

- ☞ 6.4 percent were five-person households;

- ☞ 2.2 percent were six-person households;

- ☞ 1.2 percent were households with seven or more persons;

- ☞ the average household was made up of 2.56 people.

Sliding Scales

When it comes to evaluating where Washington stands in the category of healthiest states, one has to wonder what happened between 2005 and 2006. In 2005, Washington ranked as the 13th healthiest state but in 2006 dropped to the 20th position.

DID YOU KNOW?

There are so many cell phones in the western portion of Washington that there weren't enough new phone numbers to meet the demand. As a result, the "564" area code was established for new phone numbers only. Existing phone lines in the area have remained connected to their original area codes.

Homeownership by Race

Here's how it all shaped up in 2005:

Race	Percentage owning homes
White	72.7
White, non-Hispanic	75.8
African American	48.2
Other races	59.2
Native American, Aleut, Eskimo	58.2
Asian or Pacific Islander	60.1
Hispanic	49.5
Non-Hispanic	71.2

(According to the U.S. Census Bureau: "The homeownership rate is the percentage of home owning households among all households in the given demographic group.")

Raising Children

If you think you only need love to raise a child, think again. Families with even the most modest income spent a considerable portion of it on their children. Here's what the statistics say:

☞ A family earning an average of $26,900 gross per year will spend $7300 each year on a child aged 0 to 2 years. That amount increases over the years, and by the ages of 15 to 17, that same family spends about $8290 on the same child.

☞ A family earning an average of $57,400 gross per year will spend $10,220 of their annual income on that infant to toddler, and by the time he or she turns 15, that amount increases to $11,290 per year.

☞ A family lucky enough to gross $108,700 a year or more will spend an average of $15,190 annually on that child aged 0 to 2 years old and $16,390 on their older teens.

If you consider doubling those amounts for each child, is it any wonder why most couples these days choose to have just one or two children?

Dollar for Dollar

In 1980, the average Washingtonian could expect to earn a gross annual income of about $10,256 a year. Ten years later, that same person could expect to earn almost double that, with the average annual income being $19,268. In 2000, the average annual income jumped another $10,000 to $30,380. And in 2005, the average income was about $35,409, keeping the trend consistent.

State Average Per Capita Incomes in 2005

State	Average annual income per capita
Washington, DC	$54,985
Connecticut	$47,819
Massachusetts	$44,289
New Jersey	$43,771
New York	$40,507
Washington	**$35,409**
Montana	$29,387
New Mexico	$27,644
West Virginia	$27,215
Mississippi	$25,318

GENERAL HEALTH AND WELLNESS

Healthy Lifestyle

Washington residents tend to be healthier than citizens of other states, possibly because of the moderate weather and the exceptional opportunities for outdoor activities. The reputation Washingtonians have as being generally laid back and casual may also be a factor in their favor.

Pulling Rank

The State Health Ranking study provides insight into the overall "healthiness" of each state in the nation based on measured performance in four areas: personal behavior, community environment, health policies and outcomes. There are subdivisions within each category, and various weighting formulas are applied, but essentially, you get a sense of the "healthy" ranking of each state.

The latest report came out in 2005, and Washington's overall "healthy" score lost a few points—going from 13 to 9 (13 being the better number). Washington also decreased, then, in how it ranked against other states—going from 11th to 15th.

Translated into good news, this means Washington is the 15th healthiest state in the nation. Furthermore, it ranked among the top 10 in five of the subdivided measures. Specifically, the state has fewer smokers, a lower number of infant deaths (5.3 per 1000), a lower rate of occupational fatalities, a lower premature death rate and a lower motor vehicle death rate (this could be because of the overwhelming traffic and the fact that cars average a slower speed...but I guess this result is an upside, regardless). If one takes the last five years into account, Washington comes in as the 13th healthiest state in the nation.

DISCOVERIES AND BREAKTHROUGHS

The Scribner Shunt

Belding Scribner invented the "Scribner Shunt" in the 1960s. The device enables dialysis to be used indefinitely to treat kidney failure, and this invention has saved hundreds of thousands of lives. In 2002, Scribner was honored with the Lasker Award—essentially the American equivalent of the Nobel Prize in Medicine. His work resulted in the world's first outpatient dialysis treatment facility, based in Washington State and opened in 1962. Today it is known as the Northwest Kidney Centers. Scribner also played a key role in getting legislation on the books that required Medicare to cover dialysis treatment.

The Heart Defibrillator

Dr. Karl William Edmark, a Seattle cardiovascular surgeon, perfected the world's first heart defibrillator between 1959 and 1962. He went on to create a lightweight version with his company, Physio-Control, which in turn helped the development of Medic One, a rescue unit developed in Seattle in 1970.

Ahead of His Time

Everett attorney and Republican state legislator C.T. Roscoe sponsored a law banning the sale of cigarettes to anyone, making Washington the first state to implement such a restriction. The year? 1893. Federal courts struck down the law within the year, but the state didn't rest. It passed another cigarette prohibition law in 1907—this time making it illegal to even possess cigarettes or papers for rolling them—that stayed on the books until 1911, when it was again struck down. It took until 2006 for Washington to get the next smoking law on the books...and it was mild in comparison! It merely bans smoking in public places. Washingtonians of legal age may sell, purchase, use and possess cigarettes to their hearts' content. Oh, the irony!

OLDEST SCHOOLS

University of Washington

The 1860–61 legislative session brought with it a proposal from Arthur Denny and the Reverend Daniel Bagley, who submitted a bill to locate a territorial university in Seattle. The original 10-acre campus was donated by Denny and was housed in the downtown core. In 1895, it moved to its current, modern-day location, with the first building named Denny Hall (the name remains the same today).

Expandable Schoolhouses

One of the first buildings in the Wallingford area was Interlake School, completed in 1904. Architect James Stephens designed it to be expanded in sections as enrollment increased, and his concept was such a success that 20 more institutions were created using the same model. In fact, Green Lake Public School, built in 1903, was the first building to employ the "Model School Plan," as it was called. Interlake School operated as a schoolhouse until 1981, when it was turned over to private developers, who adapted it for retail use. It is now known as the Wallingford Center and houses many retail shops and restaurants—and yet many of its original architectural features are still intact.

Oldest Grammar School in Central Seattle

In 1905, schools in the downtown Seattle area were overcrowded with children, and the need for new buildings was huge. The First Hill area of the city was at that time largely residential, though it was going through the beginning period of transformation to business use as well. Summit School was a derivation of the "Model School Plan," and it functioned as a grammar school until its closure in 1965. Today, the building houses Seattle's Northwest School, focused on art education, and it still stands at 1415 Summit Avenue.

Nihon Go Gakko

Japanese immigrants have long been a fixture of the Seattle area, and as such, active in the communities they lived in. It was important to them to have their children learn Japanese along with English, but there was no formal program in existence, so they raised funds and started their own. The Nihon Go Gakko school was opened in 1913 at 1414 South Weller, where it still stands and operates today. The school was closed during the internment years of World War II and for a few years afterwards. It is the oldest operating Japanese language school in the continental United State.

HIGHER LEARNING

Educational Buffet

Washington provides lots of choice when it comes to education—and that even includes the possibility of attending one of the top universities in the world (the University of Washington was recently added to the top 20 list).

The State of Washington has:

- more than 400,000 college students;
- four public four-year universities;
- over 300 private university and technical schools;
- 39 four-year colleges and universities;
- 29 public two-year colleges;
- five public vocational-technical colleges;
- two new community college branch campuses opened in King County in 2006.

Every year since 1974, the University of Washington (called "UDub" locally) qualifies for more federal research funding than any other public university in the United States. Since 1991, the university has managed to place second among all U.S. universities (both public and private) receiving federal science and engineering grants. While certainly one of the top schools in the nation, the *Economist* recently ranked the institution among the world's top 20 universities—17th overall, sixth among universities worldwide in research article citations and 15th in the number of cited researchers on its faculty. One hundred eighty-eight new companies have been formed as a direct result of the University of Washington's research advances.

Trends in Education

The overall workforce in Washington ranks among the nation's top five for education, productivity and experience. Nearly one in five Seattleites has a graduate or professional degree.

The state also ranks well in terms of undergraduates. In 2004, the percentage of Washington residents age 25 or older with at least a bachelor's degree went up and beat the U.S. average.

Student-Teacher Ratios Higher Than Most

Washington lags in student-teacher ratios, ranking near the bottom in the country, at 46th. The five-year average is 19.6 students per teacher for the state.

Literacy

Seattle is considered to be the most literate city in the country. Per capita bookstore sales are nearly three times the national average.

Washington's per capita bookstore sales figure is higher than the national average, too. The state leads the country with the highest SAT scores and comes in second in the ACTs.

DIVISION OF POWER

Democrat or Republican?

Washington has been a fairly liberal state since its inception, being one of the first states to adopt women's suffrage. It has vacillated between Democrat and Republican over the years, but today the political lines are pretty obvious and essentially divide the state between east and west.

The Seattle metropolitan area is increasingly liberal and widely Democrat, while the Republican party lays claim to the majority of those on the east side of the mountains. Interestingly, this division runs counter-intuitive to economic lines. The liberal area earns the most income, and there are far more working-class folk and even poverty-level families that embrace the Republican platform. The upscale suburbs have been trending Democratic, while old blue-collar lumber country strongholds have soured on the Democrats. Seattle's King County, by a wide margin the most affluent county in the state, is also its liberal stronghold: 65 percent voted for John Kerry in 2004, with a popular vote margin of 279,000, the sixth highest of any county in the nation. Republicans run best in the arid country east of the Cascades with far lower income levels.

Historically, Washington had never voted for a full-fledged Democrat in a presidential election until 1932 with Franklin D. Roosevelt. Up until that time, the Republican ticket generally won the state, except during the years 1896, when the populist voters called for William Jennings Bryan, and 1912, when Theodore Roosevelt won on the Progressive ticket.

Why the Democratic Party? The explanation has most to do with the influence of two Washington political leaders—Henry Jackson and Warren Magnuson—who were both active in the area politically for over 30 years.

NOTABLE FIGURES

Supreme Court Justice

William O. Douglas (1898–1980) served as a U.S. Supreme Court Justice. He in fact served one of the longest terms in the court's history—37 years. He grew up in Yakima, attended Whitman College in Walla Walla and authored dozens of books. Douglas acquired some nicknames while serving on the Supreme Court—some meant to flatter and others to insult. The best-known moniker was "Wild Bill," which he was called because he would often stand alone in his opinion on a case and he often affected cowboy-style mannerisms. He was also referred to as the "Great Dissenter" and the "Lone Ranger."

"These days I see America identified more and more with material things, less and less with spiritual standards. These days I see America acting abroad as an arrogant, selfish, greedy nation interested only in guns and dollars, not in people and their hopes and aspirations. We need a faith that dedicates us to something bigger and more important than ourselves or our possessions. Only if we have that faith will we be able to guide the destiny of nations in this the most critical period of world history."

–William O. Douglas, *This I Believe*, National Public Radio broadcast, 1952.

Presidential Cabinet Member

Lewis B. Schwellenbach (1894–1948) was born in Wisconsin and moved to Spokane when he was eight years old. He received his education at the University of Washington, receiving a law degree and beginning his involvement in politics. He was active in labor union law and won election to the United States Senate in 1934. He was appointed Secretary of Labor by then-President Truman, who was looking for a leader more aware of the day's issues.

Schwellenbach delivered and was more active in the role than past secretaries. In fact, he evolved the role into being more about policy making than record keeping, becoming active as a liason between unions and businesses.

Brock Adams

Brock Adams (1927–2004) first came to Washington when he attended the University of Washington as an undergraduate. After receiving his law degree at Harvard in Cambridge, Massachusetts, he returned to the Seattle area to practice law. He also served as a U.S. representative and senator. He was elected as a Democrat to the House in 1965 and served six terms. He was chairman for the Budget Committee during the 94th Congress and was thought to be on the short list for Speaker of the House, but was then appointed Secretary of Transportation for President Jimmy Carter. In 1986, Adams became a U.S. senator by defeating then-incumbent Slade Gorton. He only served one term from January 3, 1987, to January 3, 1992, as he declined to run again in 1993 because of allegations made against him publicly.

Thomas Stephen Foley

Thomas Stephen Foley (b. 1929) was born and raised in Spokane and attended undergraduate and law school at the University of Washington. He served as Speaker of the House of Representatives from 1989–95, after having been a successful member of Congress for 15 years. Under President Bill Clinton, he was made chairman of the Foreign Intelligence Advisory Board in 1996. From 1997 to 2001, he was the U.S. ambassador to Japan.

Senator Maggie

Warren G. Magnuson (1905–89) grew up in the Midwest but came to Seattle to attend the University of Washington. He stayed in the area and represented Washington in the Senate longer than anyone else—six consecutive terms (equaling 36 years)! He was a Democrat who served in the U.S. Senate from 1945 to 1981 and was chair of the Appropriations Committee. He also served as a member of the House of Representatives from 1937 to 1944. Seattle's Magnuson Park was named for him in 1977. His nickname "Maggie" was given to him by fans when he was a quarterback in high school. While he wasn't terribly fond of the moniker, it stuck, and he was known as Maggie by his Washington colleagues and constituents.

DID YOU  KNOW?

Warren Magnuson married Peggins Maddieux, the city's 1927 "Miss Seattle" beauty contest winner, in 1928. They divorced in 1935.

Senator and Potential Presidential Candidate

Henry M. Jackson (1912–83) was born and raised in Everett. He attended the University of Washington for his undergraduate degree and Stanford University in California for his graduate studies, after which he returned to his home state. He served in the House beginning in 1940 and then in the Senate beginning in 1952. Jackson unsuccessfully ran for the Democrat party presidential nomination in 1976.

Youngest Governor

Daniel J. Evans (b. 1925) was born and raised in Seattle and educated at the University of Washington. He was the youngest man ever to be elected governor of Washington and also holds the record for the most consecutive terms served (three). He later went on to the Senate, serving from 1983 to 1989. He served as president of the liberal Evergreen State College in Olympia from 1977 to 1983.

First Woman...Twice!
(And a Presidential Appointee)

Dixie Lee Ray (1914–94) was born in Tacoma. She was appointed by President Richard Nixon to chair the Atomic Energy Commission (AEC) in 1973 and was the first and only woman to serve the AEC as chair. She was also the first, and to date the only female governor that Washington has had, serving from 1977 to 1981. Additionally, she was a presidential appointee as the Assistant Secretary of State with responsibilities for

the Bureau of Oceans and the Office of International and Scientific Affairs. She had strong environmental preservation beliefs and published many books on the subject, her last in 1993 entitled *Environmental Overkill: What Ever Happened to Common Sense?* She was known to appreciate technology but also had a cautious attitude regarding how it should be applied. A quote: "The general public has long been divided into two parts—those who think science can do anything, and those who are afraid it will."

First Woman Mayor

Bertha Knight Landes (1868–1943) was the first woman ever to be elected mayor of a large American city. She won Seattle in 1926 and served until 1928.

Nation's First Chinese American Governor

Gary Locke (b. 1950) was born and raised in Seattle and served as governor of the state from 1997 to 2005. With his support, Washington raised education spending by $1 billion. A Democrat, Locke was elected to the Washington House of Representatives in 1982, during which time he was also chairman of the Appropriations Committee. In 1993, Locke became the first Chinese American to be elected County Executive of King County, and from there, ran for governor. In 2005, he decided against running for a third term, saying that he wanted to spend more time with his family. Some have speculated that racist threats received during his tenure influenced his decision. Locke went on to join the Seattle office of the law firm Davis Wright Tremaine, LLP.

CANADA-U.S. RELATIONS

Oregon Treaty of 1846

This treaty established the boundary between the U.S. and Canada through the Strait of Juan De Fuca at the 49th parallel, about 121 miles north of the Mississippi source. This agreement, however, took from 1792 to 1818 to establish!

The U.S. wanted to extend its territory north to 54°40' N, which resulted in the slogan "Fifty-four forty or fight!" Ironically, the Oregon Treaty's ambiguity (a line drawn through the water) led to the next dispute...

The "Pig Wars"

Officially called the San Juan Boundary Dispute, the "Pig War" was a dispute between the U.S. and Canada (Britain) about where exactly the boundary between Washington and Canada lay in the Strait of Juan de Fuca. The confusion occurred because the then-existing agreement that had come about in the Oregon Treaty of 1846 put the boundary in the middle of the body of water and did not clarify who owned the many islands that crossed the line. The pig came into play in 1859, when an American killed a pig that was owned by a British settler, who wanted compensation. Amazing the things that start wars, isn't it? It took until 1872, when outsider William I of Germany arbitrated the fight (for heaven's sake), and he "awarded" the San Juan archipelago to the U.S. The San Juan Island National Historical Park showcases relics of this fight restored within the two "camps," the American Camp and the British Camp—on opposite ends of the island!

The Treaty of Washington

This treaty on Canadian-American relations was negotiated in 1871 and stated that while Canada was allied with Britain, their relationship would not threaten Americans nor challenge U.S. supremacy in North America.

Peace Arch Park

The International Peace Arch straddles the international boundary dividing British Columbia, Canada, from Washington. The base of one side of the arch is planted in American soil, while the other rests in Canadian earth.

Historically, the arch commemorates the centennial (1814–1914) of the signing of the Treaty of Ghent on December 24, 1814, which ended the War of 1812 between the U.S. and Great Britain. The conflict involved Canadians as well as Americans and the British. In 1914, 100 years after the signing of the treaty, humanitarian and road builder Sam Hill, decided that it was a milestone he wanted recognized. With the donated services of British architect H.W. Corbett, Hill gathered together a workforce of volunteers from both sides of the border and began building a peace arch on the international boundary between Blaine, Washington, and Douglas, British Columbia. Dedicated in 1921, it was the first monument built and dedicated to world peace.

Inscribed on the American side are the words "Children of a Common Mother"; on the Canadian side the inscription reads "Brethren Dwelling Together in Unity." The interior of the west side of the arch states: "1814 Open One Hundred Years 1911," whereas the interior of the east side proclaims the wish "May These Gates Never Be Closed."

The International Peace Arch is one of the few landmarks in the world listed on the National Historic Registries of two different countries.

Here are a few facts about the United States Canada Peace Arch:

☛ The monument stands 67 feet high.

☛ The foundation consists of 76 14-inch pilings driven 25 to 30 feet into the earth.

☛ It is earthquake-proof—one of the first structures in North America able to make that claim.

☛ In total, 3500 sacks of concrete and 50 tons of steel were needed to complete the project.

☛ About 200 perennials and 55,000 annuals are planted in the park grounds surrounding the Peace Arch each year.

☛ More than 500,000 tourists visit the monument annually.

 DID YOU KNOW?

The Peace Arch commemorates the longest undefended boundary in the world.

CULTURAL MECCA

The State of the Arts

Washingtonians firmly embrace the arts, whatever form they take.

- ☛ Washington boasts higher photography store sales per capita than the national average.

- ☛ The motion picture per capita spending is higher in Washington than in other states (Seattle is even higher— in 2004, Seattle residents went to the movies approximately 61 percent more frequently than the national average).

- ☛ Museum and art gallery per capita sales are significantly higher in most areas of the state than in other parts of the country.

- ☛ Jobs considered part of the "creative economy" grew more than three times faster than the national average in Seattle– King County.

- ☛ Seattle has the third largest theater community in the United States, lagging only behind New York and Chicago.

Lack of Funding

Interestingly, though, while residents of Washington clearly embrace the arts wholeheartedly, the state lags behind in actual arts funding. In fact, while per capita arts funding increased slightly in 2005, it is still far behind the national average—so much so that the state's five-year average funding put it into 40th place in the nation. Not so good, really.

Art in Public Places

The state requires that when particular state-funded buildings are constructed, one-half of one percent of construction costs must be used to buy public art. The Washington State Arts Commission administers a process by which the people who live and work in the area actually get to make the decisions about the artwork selected. It works like this: agencies eligible for the public art funding appoint a five- to seven-member art selection team. The Art in Public Places (AIPP) group then directs that team, which usually includes local residents and artists as well as building users and staff. Even the architect sometimes gets involved as team advisor. The artwork that the team eventually chooses becomes part of the State Art Collection, though it is housed and maintained by the facility where the artwork lives.

Art in the Schools

Washington is one of the only states to acquire artwork for its public schools and has been doing so now for 31 years. In 2005, a virtual exhibition was created to commemorate the 30th anniversary of the program, highlighting a commissioned works of art from each year of the 30-year span. The exhibition can be viewed online at www.arts.wa.gov.

Just two examples of art in schools:

- ☞ White River School District houses 25 artworks for the state collection, including creations by local artists Marita Dingus and Cappy Thompson. You can see the art at Foothills Elementary, Glacier Middle School, White River High, White River Middle School and Wilkeson Elementary.

- ☞ Washington State University and its myriad branch campuses house 46 pieces of art for the state collection, including pieces by Montana artist John Buck and local artist Robert Maki.

DID YOU KNOW?

According to a UNESCO study on international flows of cultural goods from 1980 to 1998: "Trade in cultural goods has grown exponentially over the last two decades. Between 1980 and 1998, annual world trade of printed matter, literature, music, visual arts, cinema, photography, radio, television, games and sporting goods surged from US\$95,340 million to US\$387,927 million."

PHOTOGRAPHERS, PAINTERS AND SCULPTORS

Edward Sheriff Curtis (1868–1952)

A photographer and ethnologist from Seattle, Edward Sheriff Curtis spent over 30 years photographing and documenting Native American tribes west of the Mississippi—over 80 of them. This enormous project resulted in his work *The North American Indian*, which consists of 20 volumes. Each one included 300 pages of text and 75 handpressed photogravures. Additional photogravure portfolios were also published as additions to each volume. Theodore Roosevelt was so moved by Curtis' work that he wrote the foreword to the first volume of the series.

Asahel Curtis (1874–1941)

The brother of Edward Sheriff Curtis, Asahel Curtis is considered the most famous Seattle photographer of the 20th century. Asahel enjoyed capturing nature, industry and early city life, whereas Edward focused primarily on Native Americans. What launched Asahel's career and solidified his place in history was his coverage of the Klondike Gold Rush; he lived with the men and photographed their experiences for two years. Today, the Asahel Curtis Photo Company photographs are an important part of the University of Washington Library collection and total 1677 items. They comprise one of the most comprehensive photographic records of Seattle, Washington State, Alaska and the Klondike from the 1850s through 1940.

Imogen Cunningham (1883–1976)

Imogen Cunningham was born in Portland, Oregon, studied at the University of Washington and later worked for Edward Curtis Studios, learning the technique of platinum printing. She went on to become a famous and successful photographer, traveling the world and taking photos of Hollywood personalities for the likes of *Vanity Fair* magazine. In 1967, she was elected a Fellow of the National Academy of Arts and Sciences; in 1968, she received an honorary Doctor of Fine Arts degree from the California College of Arts and Crafts, Oakland; and in 1970, she was awarded a Guggenheim Fellowship to print from her early negatives. On her 90th birthday, she was honored with the title "Artist of the Year" by the San Francisco Art Commission, and the Metropolitan Museum of New York held an exhibition of her work.

Mark Tobey (1890–1976)

Mark Tobey was an abstract painter who lived in Seattle off and on throughout his adult life. His works have been compared to Jackson Pollock's in style, though they preceded Pollock's work by more than a decade. His paintings can be found in fine and modern art museums all over the world. Tobey was good friends with Seattle's legendary restaurant owner Ivar Hagland.

Robert Motherwell (1915–91)
Considered one of the founders of abstract expressionism, Robert Motherwell was born and raised in Washington. He is perhaps best known for a body of work done in black and white, called *Elegy to the Spanish Republic*, which includes over 100 canvases and cites the Spanish Civil War as its inspiration. His work is known and exhibited internationally.

Dudley C. Carter (1891–1992)

Known for his enormous wood sculptures, Dudley C. Carter generally depicted Native American scenes. He was born in British Columbia, but entered a soap-carving contest in Seattle two years running that landed him free tuition at the Art Institute and brought him to the city. His primary tool was an ax, and his works are on display across the Pacific Northwest, including Washington, Oregon and California. He is known internationally as well, and some of his art is housed in Japan and Germany.

Many of Carter's techniques were learned from aboriginal tribes when he was a child. Most fascinating is the fact that he was the first King County, Washington Parks and Recreation artist in residence—at the ripe old age of 96!

George Tsutakawa (1910–97)

George Tsutakawa was a Seattle painter, sculptor and fountain maker of wide repute. His fountains, in particular, dot the Seattle and Washington landscape—you can visit the Naramore Fountain at Sixth Avenue and Seneca Street in downtown Seattle. Tsutakawa has more than 75 major bronze fountain sculptures on display in public spaces across the U.S., Japan and Canada. He was recognized with two honorary doctorate degrees from Whitman College and Seattle University. Additionally, the Emperor of Japan and the National Japanese American Citizen's League paid homage with achievement awards.

Dale Chihuly (b. 1941)

A world famous glass sculptor from Tacoma, Dale Chihuly's 25,000-square-foot studio is located on Seattle's Lake Union. His glass artwork is celebrated throughout the world and is a permanent fixture in many museum collections. Special exhibitions that have piqued public interest include *Chihuly Over Venice* and *New York Botanical Gardens*.

MUSIC

Washington Puts Its Money Where Its Ears Are

Washington's per capita music store spending is higher than the national average, and Seattle–King County's per capita spending on musical instruments and supplies is significantly higher, coming in at $37 compared to the national average of just $23. The city of Seattle almost doubled the national average, with per capita music store sales 1.9 times the national average, at $44. This could have something to do with the number of talented musicians that hail from the area.

Bing

Harry Lillis Crosby (1904–77) was born in Tacoma and later moved to Spokane before he became famous as Bing Crosby. He was one of the most famous musicians in history, and his work is said to have influenced many greats that followed him, including Frank Sinatra. He spent much time overseas entertaining, and in a poll following World War II, he was voted the number one person who did the most for GI morale. In winning the title, he beat out FDR, General Dwight Eisenhower and even the renowned armed forces entertainer Bob Hope (ironically, one of Crosby's best friends). To further underscore Crosby's popularity and

fame, in 1948, he was voted the most admired person alive—putting him ahead of Sinatra, Jackie Robinson (the baseball great) and even the Pope!

WHITE CHRISTMAS

Crosby's biggest hit song was his rendition of Irving Berlin's "White Christmas," broadcast on the radio during the 1941 Christmas season and performed by Crosby in the movie *Holiday Inn.* The song was number one on the charts for 11 weeks in 1941 and hit the top 30 charts another 16 times over the years—even taking number one again in 1945 and January 1947. To this day, the song is still the bestselling holiday single and the second-bestselling song ever. Crosby is on the short list of the biggest record sellers of all time, a list that includes Frank Sinatra, Johnny Mathis, Elvis Presley and the Beatles. A full 23 of his albums went gold and platinum, but consider this—gold and platinum records didn't exist until after Bing retired in 1958.

HE CAN ACT, TOO!

This multi-talented Washingtonian didn't stop with just these accomplishments, though. Crosby was also an actor, and he established himself as one of the very best. He was the third most popular actor of all time, behind only Clark Gable and John Wayne according to ticket sales. Furthermore, Crosby is tied for second place on the "All Time Number One Stars" list with three other actors: Clint Eastwood, Tom Hanks and Burt Reynolds, according to Quigley Publishing Company's *International Motion Picture Almanac.* Beyond mere popularity, Crosby was critically recognized as a great thespian, winning an Academy Award as Best Actor for *Going My Way* in 1944 and kudos for his role as an alcoholic entertainer in *The Country Girl* in 1954.

DID YOU KNOW?

The *Village Voice* published a biography of Bing Crosby in 2001 that mentioned his love of marijuana, claiming he smoked it in his early career and that, along with his friend Louis Armstrong, he advocated for its decriminalization in the 1960s and 1970s.

A Star is Born

Patrice Munsel (b. 1925) was the youngest singer ever to sign a Metropolitan Opera contract, making the cover of *Time* magazine in 1951. She was born in Spokane, but sensing her great talent, her family moved her to New York City to study opera at the age of 15. Under the tutelage of her opera coach Giacomo Spadoni, who was the chorus master of the Met, she was signed by the time she was 17. Maestro Spadoni went on to Hollywood to work with Kathryn Grayson and Mario Lanza. Munsel had a TV series as well, which ran from 1956 to 1957, called *The Patrice Munsel Show.*

"Q"

Quincy Jones (b. 1933) was born in Chicago but moved to Bremerton when he was 10. He was involved in the music scene from a young age and was friends with the young Ray Charles, who lived in Seattle for a time, too. Jones is a man of many talents—jazz musician, composer, film producer, record label owner and entertainment company owner. As such, he has made a huge impact on the world of entertainment and opened doors repeatedly for African American entertainers. He has written the scores for 33 (thus far) movies, along with many popular TV shows, including *Sanford and Son* and the *The Bill Cosby Show*. His first film venture was in co-producing *The Color Purple* with Steven Spielberg, the movie that introduced Whoopi Goldberg and Oprah Winfrey to American audiences. He is currently the most nominated Grammy artist ever, with a total of 76 nominations and 26 awards. He has also been honored with an Emmy Award, seven Oscar nominations, and the Academy of Motion Picture Arts and Sciences Jean Hersholt Humanitarian Award.

The "Wild Man of Borneo"

Jimi Hendrix (1942–70) is widely considered one of the greatest musicians in the history of rock and roll. Born and raised in Seattle, he dropped out of high school and became a paratrooper in the military for a short time, until he decided to pursue music as a career. While playing in New York City clubs, he met English musician Chas Chandler, who loved his sound and convinced him that he needed to move to London. He did, forming the band the Jimi Hendrix Experience, which included drummer Mitch Mitchell and bassist Noel Redding. Their first performance was in Paris in 1966, and the rest, as they say, is history. People loved the music. So much so that when they released their first album *Are You Experienced?* in 1967, it became an instant hit. In fact, one of Hendrix's most famous songs, "Purple Haze," was included on that first album. He went on to form another band and release more albums, but he was destined for a short life. Hendrix died in 1970, just 27 years old, after overdosing on barbiturates and then choking on his own vomit.

Sisters of Rock

Ann and Nancy—the Wilson sisters—of the band Heart, found their first successes in Vancouver, BC, where they were living so that band member Mike Fisher could avoid the draft.

Mushroom Records released their first album, *Dreamboat Annie*, in 1975. It became an instant success in Canada and proved to be in the U.S. as well. Two hits came from that album that eventually went on to sell a million copies. Their next hit came in 1977 with *Barracuda*, which sold a million-plus copies again and launched them firmly as rock stars.

 On the 11th anniversary of grunge musician Kurt Cobain's death, his hometown of Aberdeen put up a memorial sign to him. Attached to the "Welcome to Aberdeen" sign are now the words "Come As You Are," which was one of Nirvana's (Cobain's band's) hit songs.

Leadbelly and H.R. Pufnstuf

Kurt Cobain (1967–94) founded the band Nirvana, whose grunge style defined the American music scene of the 1990s and brought the focus of the nation to Seattle's bands. Originally from Aberdeen, a town in a coastal part of the state, Cobain eventually moved to Olympia, where he and high school friend Chris Novoselic kicked Nirvana into high gear. Nirvana's first album *Bleach* was released in 1989 by the Seattle "indie" label Sub Pop Records. The band replaced drummer Chad Channing with Dave Grohl and headed into 1991. Everything changed with the success of their new album, *Nevermind*. Handled by well-known industry label Geffen, the album rocketed the band to international fame.

Overwhelmed by Fame

Unfortunately, fame wasn't something that Cobain was prepared for. Having been something of a rebel and fringe follower throughout his life, the media attention bothered him immensely. Cobain suffered from depression, drug abuse and a chronic stomach condition that kept him in almost constant pain. After almost overdosing on tour, Kurt holed up at home in Seattle and allegedly committed suicide in 1994, though there are some who believe his death was actually murder. Several movies and books have probed the evidence and asked questions, with the goal of having the case reopened by the Seattle Police Department (Cobain was living in the Seattle neighborhood of Lake Washington at the time of his death).

Cobain's Legacy

Two other bands that found massive success during Seattle's grunge heyday of the 1990s were Soundgarden and Pearl Jam—it's hard to say if either would have found their audience so easily had it not been for Cobain and Nirvana. Oh, and what's that about Leadbelly and H.R. Pufnstuf? Those were just two of Cobain's major musical influences.

DID YOU KNOW?

Both Kurt Cobain and Jimi Hendrix had an enormous impact during their four-year musical careers, both were 27 years old when they died of drug overdoses, and both were left-handed guitar players from Seattle. Trippy, huh?

Death Cab for Cutie

Ben Gibbard formed his band Death Cab for Cutie in Bellingham in 1997, and they've been upwardly mobile ever since. Their first hit album was *Transatlanticism*, released in October 2003, and it sold 225,000 copies in the first year. Singles from the album continue to find their way into pop culture—from the soundtracks of hit TV shows *The O.C.* and *Six Feet Under* to the movies *The Wedding Crashers* and *Mean Creek*. In November 2004, Death Cab signed a deal with Atlantic Records and promptly released two singles, "Soul Meets Body" and "Crooked Teeth," followed by the full album *Plans* in August 2005. The album received a Grammy Award nomination for Best Alternative Album of 2005.

A live version of Death Cab for Cutie's song "Photobooth" is included on the soundtrack of the Xbox 360 game *Project Gotham Racing 3*.

ARCHITECTURE

Timeless Apartments

Frederick William Anhalt (1896–1996), known simply as "Fred," designed many apartment buildings on Seattle's Capitol Hill. He was largely influenced by Norman and Tudor designs, and this is evident in his work—many of his buildings look like grand estates or mini-castles. Most of his landmark buildings are still in use and fetch a premium when sold.

Mansions, Hotels and Country Clubs

Kirtland Kelsey Cutter (1860–1939) was Spokane's primary architect from 1888 to 1923, during which time he designed the Davenport Hotel (still a major city landmark), the Spokane Club and many large abodes for the city's wealthiest citizens. He did additional work west of the mountains in Seattle, designing several Seattle mansions (such as Stimson-Green on Capitol Hill), country clubs (such as the Seattle Golf and Country Club with partner architect Karl Gunnar Malmgren) and the original wing of the Rainier Club in the downtown core.

World Trade Center Designer

Minoru Yamasaki (1912–86) was born in Seattle as a second-generation Japanese American. He designed the World Trade Center in New York City, whose two main towers were destroyed and immortalized in the September 11, 2001, terrorist attacks on the U.S. He also designed the Century Plaza Towers in Los Angeles, the Pacific Science Center in Seattle and the Dharan International Airport in Saudi Arabia, along with many other well-known public buildings internationally.

Hollywood Farm

Sitting on what is currently the Chateau St. Michelle Winery
in Woodinville is historic Hollywood Farm. It was built by
Frederick S. Stimson, an early Seattle resident who made his
fortune in the lumber industry. He started the farm in 1910 as
a retreat from the city, but moved there full time in 1918 and
dedicated himself to breeding prize-winning Holstein dairy
cows. He also started a summer camp for children, called the
Hollywood Fresh Air Farm, where 20 underprivileged youths
would come up from Seattle and stay on the farm for two weeks,
eating a farm-fresh diet and enjoying the outdoors. The structure
was listed on the National Register of Historic Places in 1978.

Seattle's Oldest Theater

Fans of theater and cultural events even in 1907, Seattle residents came out in droves to take in the Moore Theater on opening night. Designed by architect E.W. Houghton, it was known
for its opulence and exceptional acoustics. The Moore is still in
operation today.

Ye College Inn

Washingtonians can still enjoy a beer at the pub inside this
nearly 100-year-old hotel and café at 4000 University Way
Northeast. Originally created as a place for guests of the 1909
Alaska-Yukon-Pacific Exposition, it was strategically placed near
the main entrance to the fairgrounds by real estate developer
Charles Cowen—who also put up a billboard advertising new
lots for sale nearby. It is the only building known to exist that
was connected to the AYP Exposition.

The Carnegie Largesse

Andrew Carnegie, the great American philanthropist, provided
funding for the building of over 1500 libraries in the United
States. Carnegie funded 43 libraries that were built across

Washington State. Only eight are still standing and seven are still used as libraries. The Clark County Historical Museum in Vancouver now uses its historical Carnegie library space. Six remain in Seattle, located in West Seattle, Greenlake, University, Queen Anne, Columbia City and Fremont, and were all recently rehabilitated. The final operating Carnegie library structure is in Ritzville about 60 miles outside of Spokane.

King Street Station
The tallest building in the city when it was completed in 1906, the King Street railway station stands at 225 feet tall. The neo-classical structure was conceived as an imitation of the Piazza San Marco in Venice, Italy, but went through a modernization-gone-wrong in the 1960s that drywalled in the original architecture. Phase one of a restoration project is expected to be complete in 2007.

Largest Building in the World
One might assume this title would be held by a structure in New York City, maybe Rome or even Paris. However, the distinction of the world's single largest building by volume goes to the Boeing Assembly Plant in Everett, where they build the model 747, 767 and 777 airplanes. Its volume totals 472 million cubic feet, or more than 98 acres of space. A tourist attraction in its own right, 140,000 visitors tour the plant each year.

Northgate, The World's First Mall
The first shopping center in the nation to be known as a "mall" was built in Seattle in 1950 and named Northgate. It had a double row of stores facing each other across a covered pedestrian walkway. There were 18 stores at launch, compared to today, when the count is well over 100. Northgate was designed by Seattle architect John Graham Jr., who was later commissioned to create the Tacoma Mall and Southcenter Mall, both still in existence and much expanded.

LITERATURE

Washington's First Pulitzer

Vernon Louis Parrington (1871–1929) was the first Washingtonian to win a Pulitzer Prize, which he did in 1928 for his two-volume work *Main Currents in American Thought* (a third volume for the series was published posthumously). The books provide portraits of key thinkers of the time along with analysis regarding the evolution of ideas that occurred over the time periods studied. His *Main Currents* books delve into three phases of American intellectual history: Calvinistic pessimism, romantic optimism and mechanistic pessimism.

The Blood of Poets

Seattle-born Audrey May Wurdemann (1911–60) was awarded a Pulitzer Prize for poetry in 1934 for *Bright Ambush*. At the age of 23, she was the youngest person ever to receive the award. Interestingly, she came from literary "stock," as it were, being the great-great-granddaughter of Percy Bysshe Shelley. Wurdemann and her husband, poet Joseph Auslander (1897–1970), often wrote short stories and novels together. Her husband was famous in his own right, becoming the first Poet Laureate of the U.S. from 1937 to 1941 and Consultant in English Poetry at the Library of Congress.

One Irish Firecracker

Mary McCarthy (1912–89) wrote *Memories of a Catholic Girlhood* in 1957. She had a troubled young childhood and was taken in by her maternal grandparents, who had deep roots in the Seattle community. In fact, her grandfather was Harold Preston, attorney and co-founder of the law firm known today as Preston Gates and Ellis, LLP (Bill Gates' father was also a later partner). In addition to nonfiction, she wrote novels and was quite politically active. Her first novel was titled *The Company She Keeps*, and while it won much critical praise, it was also considered scandalous as it depicted the New York intellectual scene of the late 1930s quite openly (think liquor and sex). In 1963, her novel *The Group* was a huge success, managing to ride the *New York Times* bestseller list for almost two years. Something of a firecracker, she had an ongoing politically based feud with writer Lillian Hellman, which allegedly was the basis for Nora Ephron's play *Imaginary Friends*. McCarthy brought the feud to the public eye in 1979, saying "every word [Hellman] writes is a lie, including 'and' and 'the,'" as a guest on *The Dick Cavett Show*. Hellman reacted violently to this statement and filed a $2.5 million libel suit against McCarthy. However, they both died before the suit was finished! I guess that's what you call a draw.

Poetry in Motion

Poet Theodore Roethke (1908–63) won a Pulitzer Prize in 1953 for his compilation *The Waking: Poems 1933–1953*. Originally from Michigan, he taught at the University of Washington from 1947 until his death in 1963. Because of the influence his works have had on generations of poets since, he is considered one of the greatest and most renowned American poets of the 20th century.

Dr. Kildare's Creator

Frederick Schiller Faust (1892–1944), a Seattle native, wrote under five pseudonyms, but is mainly now known as Max Brand. A master of the western novel, he churned out hundreds of them during his lifetime. He dabbled in many genres, including pulp and comics. For example, he developed the character of

Dr. James Kildare, who became the star character of the famous radio show *Dr. Kildare*, the comic book series and the star characters of many movies and then television series. Faust was one of the most prolific writers that ever lived. He is believed to have written between 25 million and 30 million words. He could reputedly turn out 12,000 words in a weekend!

Criminal Minds

The genre of true crime writing is said to have been established by Seattle writer Ann Rule (b. 1935). A former police officer who grew up in a family practicing law enforcement, her interest in the subject matter is certainly an honest one. She is fascinated by why someone becomes a criminal, and it is that subject she explores through her writing. Ann has worked as a true crime writer since 1969 and has authored 20 books and more than 1400 articles. Ironically, she spent time volunteering in Seattle with the infamous serial killer Ted Bundy and was actively writing articles about his crimes at the time.

Psychedelic Writer-in-Residence

The author of several books that trip the fantastic, Tom Robbins (b. 1936) is a good example of an eccentric Washington resident. Independent and wary of the limelight, Robbins lives in a small town outside Seattle and produces a book every few years or so. His most rabid fans tend to be in the stage of life where they are exploring their personalities—late adolescence and early college seem to be his sweet spot, though his work is adored by many outside his "classic" demographic.

The Man Who Learned It All in Kindergarten

Robert Fulghum (b. 1937) has published seven bestselling books, perhaps the most well-known of them all being *All I Really Need to Know I Learned in Kindergarten*. He also wrote *It Was on Fire When I Lay Down on It*, *Uh-Oh*, *Maybe (Maybe Not)*, *From Beginning to End—The Rituals of Our Lives*, *True Love* and *Words I Wish I Wrote*. There are 16 million copies of his books in print, he's been published in 27 languages in 103 countries, and he has been a Grammy nominee for the Spoken Word Award.

MEDIA AND ENTERTAINMENT

Journalistic Genius

Edward R. Murrow (1908–65), European director of CBS, broadcast from London during World War II. Murrow was born Egbert Roscoe Murrow near Greensboro, North Carolina, in a log cabin without electricity or plumbing. When he was five, his family moved to Washington State and settled in Blanchard, about 30 miles from the Canadian border. Murrow's journalistic work was influential in the field of radio journalism; in fact, he was such a well-known broadcast journalist that parts of his life were documented in the recent George Clooney movie *Good Night and Good Luck*. Murrow attended Washington State University (WSU, called WAZoo by locals), where during his second year of college, he officially changed his name from Egbert to Edward. While at WSU, he also met Ida Lou Anderson, the instructor that Murrow credited with inspiring his successful broadcasting career. Thank goodness for Ida!

DID YOU KNOW?

One of Edward R. Murrow's most famous catchphrases was "Good night and good luck," which stemmed from his London experiences while providing radio broadcast coverage of World War II. Towards the end of 1940, Germany was bombing London every night in air raids over the city, a time commonly referred to as the "Blitz." Friends and neighbors were never sure they would see each other again, so when they parted, they began saying not merely "So long," but instead "So long and good luck." One night, Murrow ended his radio broadcast segment with "Good night and good luck"—a riff on the common parting catchphrase at the time—and former WSU instructor Ida Anderson heard it, liked it and insisted he stick with it.

Friend to Hollywood

Washington is one of the top 15 film production states in the country. It has roughly 1500 related businesses that employ about 5000 Washingtonians, who produce feature films, television movies, series or episodes, commercials, documentaries, industrial films and music videos. Out-of-state producers make over 100 film and video projects in Washington every year, contributing more than $40 million to the state's economy annually. Another $45 million is generated by in-state film and video companies, bringing the total annual economic impact to about $100 million. Certainly not pocket change!

A Selection of Movies Filmed in Washington

And here just a selected list of some of the films that have been made in Washington:

The Butterfly Effect (2004)

Frasier (TV, 1993–2004)

Agent Cody Banks (2003)

The Bachelorette (2003)

The Core (2003)

The Diary of Ellen Rimbauer (TV, 2003)

A Guy Thing (2003)

Enough (2002)

The Hunted (2002)

Life or Something Like It (2002)

The Ring (2002)

Rose Red (2002)

Shell Seekers (2002)

Whacked! (2002)

e-Dreams (2001)

The Fugitive (TV 2000–01)

Highway (2001)

The Immigrant Garden (2001)

Love 'n' Hate (2001)

Dancer in the Dark (2000)

Get Carter (2000)

Men of Honor (2000)

Nowheresville (2000)

Rock Star (2001)

Austin Powers 2: The Spy Who Shagged Me (1999)

Boy Wonderz (1999)

Cage the Dog (1999)

Double Jeopardy (1999)

The Engagement Party (1999)

Lovers Lane (1999)

Mel (1999)

Revenge of Mama Sue (1999)

Snow Falling on Cedars (1999)

10 Things I Hate About You (1999)

Detour (1998)

Practical Magic (1998)

Under Heaven (1998)

Black Circle Boys (1997)

Bobby & Rachel (1997)

Dante's Peak (1997)

Love Always (1997)

The Postman (1997)

Prefontaine (1997)

Rough Crossing (TV 1997)

The Sixth Man (1997)

Black Sheep (1996)

Fear (1996)

From Dusk Till Dawn (1996)

The Last of the High Kings (1996)

The Long Kiss Goodnight (1996)

Murder, She Wrote (1984–96)

Free Willy 2: The Adventure Home (1995)

Mad Love (1995)

"Northern Exposure" (TV 1990–95)

Benny & Joon (1993)

Sleepless in Seattle (1993)

The Hand That Rocks the Cradle (1992)

Twin Peaks, (TV 1990–91)

Die Hard 2: Die Harder (1990)

The Hunt For Red October (1990)

Indiana Jones and the Temple of Doom (1984)

An Odyssey of the North (1914)

The Deer Hunter (1978)

MacArthur (1977)

Lost Horizon (1973)

Sometimes a Great Notion (1972)

It Happened at the World's Fair (1963)

The Hanging Tree (1959)

The Lusty Men (1952)

Lassie Home Home (1943)

Beyond the Line of Duty (1942)

The Call of the Wild (1935)

Here Comes the Navy (1934)

Courage of Lassie (1946)

Tacoma Narrows Bridge Collapse (1940)

Tugboat Annie (1933)

The Grub Stake (1923)

A Romance of Seattle (1919)

The Lure of Alaska (1915)

An Odyssey of the North (1914)

First Avenue, Seattle, Washington (1897)

Loading Baggage for Klondike (1897)

SS Queen Leaving Dock (1897)

SS Queen Loading (1897)

SS Williamette Leaving for Klondike (1897)

Merce Cunningham (b. 1919)

Born in Washington, Merce Cunningham studied dance at the
Cornish College of the Arts in Seattle, Washington. His specialty is modern dance, and he owns his own company—the
Merce Cunningham Dance Company. He has choreographed
over 150 works and presented them all over the world.
Cunningham has also worked with many world-renowned theater groups, including the New York City Ballet and the Paris
Opera Ballet. He has been the recipient of many awards,
including the Kennedy Center Honors for lifetime achievement
in 1985 and the National Medal of Arts in 1990. He has been
inducted into the Hall of Fame at the National Museum of
Dance, and for his 75th birthday, New York City's mayor
declared April 16, 1994, to be "Merce Cunningham Day."

Robert Joffrey (1930–88)

Robert Joffrey was born in Seattle and studied dance in New
York City. A talented choreographer, Joffrey gained fame for his
modern ballets. He formed his own dance company in 1954,
moved it to Los Angeles in 1982 and then to Chicago with
a name change to the Joffrey Ballet of Chicago in 1995.

Relax and Laugh a Little

Gary Larson is the comic strip artist of *Far Side* fame, first
published in 1979 by the *Seattle Times* and syndicated in 1980.
Born in Tacoma and a lifelong Seattle-area resident, Larson
credits much of his success to a happy childhood. His work was
recognized by the National Cartoonist Society Newspaper Panel
who bestowed their Cartoon Award on Larson in 1985 and
1988, and their Reuben Award in 1990 and 1994. He was recognized for his unique strips by the National Cartoonist Society
in 1989, 1990, 1991, 1993 and 1995. He is now retired.

Memories for Every Child of a "Certain Age"

The character of Julius Pierpont, aka J.P. Patches, who looked something like a homeless Ronald McDonald, was played by Chris Wedes from 1958 to 1981. The television show named after him was one of the longest-running children's TV shows in American history. J.P. was an eccentric clown whose nonsense delighted children. He "lived" in the dump, wore crazy patchwork clothes and had a "girlfriend" named Gertrude who was obviously a man in makeup and a wig (though J.P. didn't know it). Key show characters included Esmerelda, Ketchikan, Grandpa Tick-Tock and Ggoorrsstt, the Friendly Frpl. The dawn of cable TV brought an end to the show, 23 years after it began.

The 10 steps to being a Patches Pal:
1. Mind Mommy and Daddy
2. Wash your hands, face, neck and ears
3. Comb your hair
4. Brush your teeth
5. Drink your milk
6. Eat all of your food
7. Say your prayers
8. Share your toys
9. Put your toys away
10. Hang up your clothes

Perhaps the show should be brought back...

Frances Farmer (1913–70)

Frances Elena Farmer was born in Seattle and went on to star in two major Hollywood films. In 1936, she was cast opposite Bing Crosby in *Rhythm on the Range*. Later that same year (a very good year for Frances), she also appeared in *Come and Get It*, based on the novel by Edna Ferber. Over the next few years, she worked on a few more movies and plays. She was married, divorced and then began to suffer from mental health problems, which sadly landed her in and out of institutions for years to come.

 Nirvana included the song "Frances Farmer Will Have Her Revenge on Seattle" on their album *In Utero*. Also, Courtney Love wore a vintage dress that had belonged to Farmer in her wedding to Kurt Cobain.

DID YOU  KNOW?

Washington is an entertainment industry mecca. More than 90 feature length films have been shot in Washington since 1999, more than 170 television events were filmed (movies, series, news), 17 music videos were made...the list goes on. In total, the industry—both local and out of town—used Washington as a location almost 700 times.

Diamond Girl

Carol Channing was born on January 31, 1921, in Seattle. Most famous for two roles, Lorelei Lee in *Gentlemen Prefer Blondes* and Dolly Gallagher Levi in *Hello, Dolly!* Claiming she is of African-American descent on her father's side, she says he kept his roots a secret throughout his life. She unveiled this in her 2002 autobiography.

Being Batman

Adam West, born William West Anderson on September 19, 1928, in Walla Walla, is best known for playing the role of Batman on the first *Batman* TV series, which ran from 1966 to 1968.

DID YOU  KNOW?

Adam West was a well-educated guy. He went to Lakeside School (the same high school as Bill Gates) and then graduated from Whitman, majoring in literature and psychology. Holy Toledo, Batman!

Dyan Cannon

Dyan Cannon was born Samile Diane Friesen on January 4, 1937, in Tacoma. She has received two Oscar nominations for Best Supporting Actress, one for *Bob and Carol and Ted and Alice* (1969) and another for *Heaven Can Wait* (1978). She became Cary Grant's fourth wife in 1965 and had a child; the couple divorced within 18 months.

Million Dollar Baby

Hilary Ann Swank was born on July 30, 1974, in Lincoln, Nebraska, and grew up in Bellingham. She has won two Academy Awards. The first Oscar was given for her portrayal of Brandon Teena in the movie *Boys Don't Cry* (1999), in which she played a young, trans-gendered teen living life as a boy. Her second Oscar was earned for her role as Maggie Fitzgerald in *Million Dollar Baby* (2004)—a professional woman boxer played opposite the legendary Clint Eastwood. Swank's success has not been easily achieved. Not only did she struggle financially growing up, but she also suffers from Attention Deficit Hyperactivity Disorder (ADHD), which she treats with Ritalin.

DID YOU KNOW?

Hilary Swank's parents separated when she was a teenager, and her mom, who knew her daughter's love for acting, moved them to Los Angeles, California. There they lived in her car until Swank's mother could afford an apartment. Swank started going to South Pasadena High and began her acting career, landing small parts in television shows such as *Growing Pains*, which enabled her to help pay the rent.

"I don't know what I did in this life to deserve this. I'm just a girl from a trailer park who had a dream." –Hilary Swank, after winning the Academy Award for *Million Dollar Baby*.

INVENTIONS AND DISCOVERIES

Sail the Oceans Blue

Wilbert McLeod Chapman (1910–70) was an internationally known ichthyologist (a scientist who studies fish) who was fascinated with the waters of the Pacific Northwest. He called himself a "biopolitician" and played an influential role in creating the Pacific Oceanic Fishery Investigations in Hawaii. This effort helped establish oceanography as a legitimate part of the scientific community.

While in the middle of a research project on the Grand Coulee Dam, Wilbert Chapman was pulled over as a murder suspect in Leavenworth on his way home one night. Evidently, there had been a murder in the area, and the police noticed blood leaking from the trunk of his car. It was, of course, from dead salmon that he had been collecting at the dam, but the police didn't buy his story. Luckily, the man in charge of the project was in Leavenworth at the time and was able to convince the police that Chapman wasn't a dangerous criminal—merely a biologist and state employee.

The Lake Washington Ship Canal

Hiram M. Chittenden (1858–1917) was an army engineer who came to Seattle as the District Engineer with the U.S. Army Corps of Engineers. His work was key to Seattle's decision to build the Lake Washington Ship Canal—what is popularly known today as the "Ballard Locks" (their formal name is the Hiram M. Chittenden Locks). They were developed to make transportation of goods more efficient by allowing the easier passage of large container vessels.

Donation of "Self" to Science

Barney Clark (1910–84) was a retired
Seattle dentist, who at 61 years of age had
heart disease so advanced that he needed
help to get to the dinner table. He
donated himself to science and became
the first recipient of an artificial heart.
He lived for 112 days following the
operation, which was considered
a huge success and paved
the way for artificial
heart advancements.

Xerography

The next time you wan-
der over to your photocopy
machine to duplicate a docu-
ment, remember to think of
good old Chester Carlson. As a
young man back in 1937, the
Washington law student is cred-
ited with having developed xerography—a Greek word for the
term "dry writing." The mimeograph machine was already
available at the time, but Carlson is said to have been annoyed
with how slow that process was. Xerography was a new process,
one that used an electrostatic process.

Still, it didn't take off right away. In fact, IBM and the U.S.
Army Signal Corps both turned Carlson down when he
approached them to invest in his idea. It took eight years of
pounding the pavement before the Xerox Corporation, then
known as the Haloid Company, came on board. And the rest,
as they say, is history.

Fish Farm Trout

Dr. Lauren Donaldson (1903–98) was a well-known ichthyologist (like Wilbert Chapman) who moved to Seattle to accept a teaching position at the University of Washington during the Great Depression. In the mid-1900s, he developed a variety of rainbow trout specifically for the food industry, where fish are raised entirely on fish farms and hatcheries. His strain of rainbow trout have continued to perform well at farms around the globe.

Zoologist Extraordinaire

Trevor Kincaid (1872–1970) was born in Peterborough, Ontario, Canada, and moved to Olympia when he was 17 years old. He was a University of Washington zoology professor who discovered many new species. As a testament to his discoveries, there are 47 plants and animals named after Kincaid. He was also known for his research on oyster culture, and his work helped create the Japanese oyster industry at Willapa Harbor.

The Father of Modern Apple Storage

Archie Van Dozen (1906–86) was a professor, horticulturist and cattleman best known as the father of controlled atmosphere storage for apples, which involves the careful control of temperature, oxygen, carbon dioxide and humidity, and allows apples to remain fresh for up to 12 months. Washington has the largest capacity of such storage of any growing region in the world, allowing people across the world to enjoy fresh Washington apples year round.

Nobel Prize Winners Affiliated with Washington State

2004: Linda B. Buck shared the Nobel Prize in Physiology or Medicine with Richard Axel for their work on olfactory receptors. Buck was born in Seattle in 1947. Her father was an electrical engineer and an inventor, which may have led to her interest in the sciences. After many years spent in New York and Boston, she returned to Seattle in 2002 as a researcher at the Fred Hutchinson Cancer Research Center.

2001: Leland H. Hartwell shared the Nobel Prize in Physiology or Medicine with Paul Nurse and Tim Hunt for contributions to the understanding of the cell cycle. Hartwell is president and director of the world-renowned Fred Hutchinson Cancer Research Center in Seattle.

1994: Martin Rodbell shared the Nobel Prize in Physiology or Medicine with Alfred G. Gilman for their discovery of G-proteins and the role of those proteins in signal transduction in cells.

1992: Edmond H. Fischer shared the Nobel Prize in Physiology or Medicine with Edwin G. Krebs for describing how reversible phosphorylation works as a switch to activate proteins and regulate various cellular processes. Fischer was born in Shanghai, China, and educated in Switzerland. He moved to Seattle in 1953 to take up a position at the University of Washington, where he met Edwin Krebs.

1990: Edward Donnall Thomas shared the Nobel Prize in Physiology or Medicine with Joseph E. Murray for the development of cell and organ transplantation. Thomas developed bone marrow transplantation as a treatment for leukemia. He taught at the University of Washington Medical School, published over 750 scholarly articles and is a researcher a the Fred Hutchinson Cancer Research Center in Seattle.

1989: Hans Georg Dehmelt, Wolfgang Paul and Norman Ramsey shared the Nobel Prize in Physics; Dehmelt and Paul for their work on ion traps and Ramsey for his invention of the separated oscillatory fields method and its use in the hydrogen maser and other atomic clocks. Dehmelt was a professor at the University of Washington from 1955 until his retirement in 2002.

1988: Washington native George H. Hitchings shared the Nobel Prize in Physiology or Medicine with Sir James Black and Gertrude Elion for their discoveries of important principles for drug treatment, Hitchings specifically for his work on chemotherapy.

1982: George Joseph Stigler won the Nobel Memorial Prize in Economics. Stigler was born in Seattle in 1911 and received his undergraduate degree from the University of Washington.

1956: Walter H. Brattain shared the Nobel Prize for Physics in 1956 for his work in developing the transistor. Brattain was born in China but grew up on a cattle ranch in Washington State. He received his undergraduate degree at Whitman College in Walla Walla.

The Dark Side of Technology

Richard Scobee (1939–86) was second in command of the Challenger's 1984 flight and logged 68 hours in space before being given command of the January 1986 mission that ended in tragedy. He was born in Cle Elum and grew up in Auburn, where the Dick Scobee Elementary School is named for him.

COMMON CRIMES

A Propensity for Burglary

While the national rate for property crime was about 3500 per 100,000 people in 2004, Washington had about 4800 the same year. For some reason, Washingtonians evidently steal more frequently than the running average. The violent crime rate, however, is significantly lower than the national average, with only 370 reported violent crimes per 100,000 versus 466 per 100,000.

Bad News on the Crime Front
A 2006 ranking of the most dangerous states to live in placed Washington in 16th spot, raising it from the 20th ranking in 2005.

DID YOU KNOW?

Hard to say if bank robbers are born or created. Either way, Washington has more than its fair share. The state ranked ninth in the nation for heists in 2005. According to crime statistics, Washington banks are most frequently robbed on Thursday afternoons between 3:00 and 6:00 PM by white males wearing hats. How's *that* for profiling?!

NOTABLE CRIMINALS

"Starvation" Heights

Dr. Linda Burfield Hazzard was a killer who got paid to murder. She began a sanatorium called Wilderness Heights in Olalla in 1907, where she claimed to cure all manner of illnesses with a combination of fasting, enemas and massage therapy. At the time, she was one of the few female doctors in the country (she was trained as an osteopath), and she presented herself as the only licensed fasting therapist. When patients grew weak (as starving people are wont to do), she convinced them to give her power of attorney and sign over their accounts. She would isolate them and continue to starve them, which often resulted in delirium and death. While all of this sounds rather unbelievable, people came from all over the world to receive her "cures." That is, until two wealthy British sisters visited, and the matter was brought to the attention of authorities because one sister managed to sneak a telegram out and ask for help. The intervention came too late for the sisters, who then each weighed about 75 pounds, but the sanatorium was shut down, and others were saved from the same fate.

The Weyerhaeuser Kidnapping

On May 24, 1935, William Dainard and Harmon Metz Waley kidnapped George Weyerhaeuser, the nine-year-old son of Tacoma lumberman J.P. Weyerhaeuser. A $200,000 ransom was collected, and the two were eventually caught. Harmon's wife Margaret and a business associate named Edward Fliss were also found to have assisted with the crime. The four of them were sentenced to a collective 135 years in prison. Only about $159,000 of the ransom was returned to the Weyerhaeusers, but the boy was unharmed. In fact, he later went on to become chairman of the board for the Weyerhaeuser Company.

Ted Bundy: Serial Killer

A handsome lawyer who was raised from a young age in Washington, Ted Bundy began a brutal killing spree in 1974, at the age of 27, that continued through 1978, when he was finally caught. It is difficult to know for sure how many girls and women he assaulted, raped and brutally murdered, but he eventually confessed to more than 30 crimes. Initially arrested in Utah, where he had moved, he was transferred to a Colorado prison because he had also committed crimes there. However, he escaped from prison twice—the second time eluding recapture. He traveled to Florida, where he went on what was his last killing spree. He was caught, tried and convicted there—and put to death in the electric chair on January 24, 1989, after many years of making appeals on death row. Were it not for a bite mark discovered on his last victim's buttocks, Ted Bundy may not have been convicted at all. The murder he was tried for in Florida that resulted in his death sentence was the only one with physical evidence proving Bundy was the perpetrator.

DID YOU KNOW?

Ted Bundy once worked as a volunteer in Seattle alongside the famous true-crime author Ann Rule—who was just starting out as a crime reporter. Oddly enough, she was covering murder stories that her colleague was committing at the time. Rule eventually wrote a biography on Bundy called *The Stranger Beside Me*.

The Green River Murderer
As if being home to one mass murderer isn't enough, Washington was also the violent playground of Gary Leon Ridgway, who has the terrible distinction of confessing to more homicides than any other serial killer in U.S. history. He began killing in 1982 and went on a spree lasting almost three years. Because many of the bodies were found in the Green River area of Washington, Ridgway became known as the "Green River Murderer."

While he had been a suspect initially in the cases, he was not arrested until almost two decades later, when enough evidence was found to support his capture. He confessed to killing 48 women. In exchange for not receiving the death penalty during his trial in 2003, he helped investigators recover the bodies of many victims that had still not been found.

Mass Murder

During the course of a robbery, 13 people were murdered at the Wah Mee Club on Maynard Alley in Seattle. The event earned this well-known gambling establishment the dubious honor of being the site of the city's worst recorded mass murder. The date of this infamous event—February 18, 1983.

Married *to* Children

Mary Kay Laterno, a 35-year-old Seattle teacher, was convicted of statutory rape of one of her 12-year-old male students back in the 1990s. After being found guilty and serving her prison sentence, she announced her nuptials to the victim, Vili Fualaau, on *Good Morning America*. Their wedding took place on April 16, 2005. The bride was 45 and the groom was 21.

KEEPING SCORE

Strike!

Seven-figure salaries aren't reserved for tennis or hockey greats. If you're good enough, you can earn that much as a bowler, too. In 1982, Earl Anthony of Tacoma proved the point by earning $1 million that calendar year. He became the first in his sport to do so.

Look Out Below!

The nation's most successful ski racer hails from Yakima. Phil Mahre earned himself a gold medal in the 1984 Olympics in downhill slalom. Tack that alongside his three World Cup over-all championship hardware, and it's an impressive collection indeed.

On Top of the World

Redmond is home to Jim Whittaker. In 1963, the mountaineer became the first American to conquer the summit of Mount Everest.

Hole in One

Golf great JoAnne Carner earned her stripes both as an amateur and as a pro. The Kirkland native was five-time U.S. champion during her amateur career and earned two U.S. Women's Open titles as a professional in 1971 and 1978.

Fancy Footwear

Talk about the end result coming down to brass tacks. In 1934, New York Giants football player Ray Flaherty thought a change in footwear would pave the way for a championship victory. The Spokane native suggested basketball shoes would provide better grip on an icy playing field. Based on the end result, Flaherty was right. New York won with a score of 30 to 13.

Making Waves

Folks keen on hydroplane racing likely know the name Ted Jones. The Seattle-born racer designed the Slo-Mo-Shun IV in 1950. The hydroplane was the first of its kind to reach speeds up to 160 miles per hour.

Fast Forward

Spokane's Tom Sneva scooped up a first place finish in the 1977 Indy 500. Along with all the kudos that comes with being number one, he added another first to his repertoire—he was the first to break 200 miles per hour during an Indy race.

New Kid on the Block

Washington was awarded its own National Basketball Association franchise on December 20, 1966. The following year, the Seattle Sonics played their first season.

Stormy First Season

The Women's National Basketball Association welcomed newbie team Seattle Storm in May 2000. An estimated 142,594 fans rooted for their team during its first season. The end result saw the team finish with a 6–26 record.

Mariner Memories

On April 6, 1977, the Seattle Mariners made their debut. The upstart team formed after Seattle's first Major League baseball team, the Pilots, folded. The Pilots floundered from 1970 to 1976. Their demise, some thought, was partly because of the lack of adequate facilities for professional sports.

Sad Beginnings

The Seattle Seahawks began their National Football League adventure on a sad note when their owner, Lloyd Nordstrom, died while vacationing in Mexico in 1976. It wasn't until 2006, after 31 seasons, that the Seahawks earned their way to a Super Bowl appearance.

FAMOUS FIRSTS

Putting Down Stakes

Explorer David Thompson is credited with establishing the first fur-trading post in Washington on behalf of the North West Company. Spokane House was built in 1810 and is thought to be the first structure erected by non-Natives in Washington.

Proud Landmark

Fort Okanogan began as little more than a single building located near the mouth of the Okanogan and Columbia Rivers. Representatives of John Jacob Astor's Pacific Fur Company founded the fort, the first "American outpost," in 1811.

Exploring a New Wilderness

The investigative expedition led by Lewis and Clark in the early part of the first decade of the 1800s was the first time non-Natives had traveled through the area on an overland route. Explorers Lewis and Clark first drew attention to the area now occupied by the small city of Vancouver in 1806 when they set up camp there. But it wasn't until 1825, when the Hudson's Bay Company established Fort Vancouver as a fur-trading post, that it was considered the first permanent white settlement in the Northwest. It became incorporated as a town on January 23, 1857. Twenty-nine years later, in 1886, the Canadian city of Vancouver, British Columbia, was incorporated. Naval explorer George Vancouver is the namesake for both these cities, making them the only major cities in each country to share a name.

Railway History

The Northern Pacific Railroad's mainline, which extended through present-day Washington, was completed in 1883.

ODDS AND ENDS

Holiday Time

Washingtonians celebrate 11 holidays each year. These holidays include those shared by other states: New Year's Day, Christmas, Thanksgiving, Veteran's Day, Labor Day, Memorial Day, Election Day and the Fourth of July. Holidays unique to the state include:

☛ January 3—Martin Luther King Jr.'s Birthday

☛ February 12—Lincoln's Birthday

☛ February (third Monday of the month)—Washington's Birthday

Is Bigger Better?
The Bank of America Tower, located in Seattle, is the tallest building in that city, hovering 1049 feet above sea level. It's so tall, in fact, that some sources call it the tallest building west of the Mississippi River.

The Ghosts of Mount Rainier

Since statistics on the topic were first collected in 1909, a total of 323 individuals have died on Mount Rainier. Of those, 65 bodies have never been recovered. But because the glacial ice that likely entombs these individuals is slowly making its way down the mountainside, chances are good one or more of these will resurface.

The first recorded disappearances on Mount Rainier, near the White River Glacier, were 50-year-old Seattle resident T.Y. Callaghan and his 30-year-old New Jersey friend Joseph W. Stevens on August 14, 1909. In that same month just two years later, Legh Osborn Garrett also went missing. It was another 35 years before the mountain claimed its largest number of single-incident victims when a Marine Corps C-46 plane crashed on the South Tahoma Glacier on December 10, 1946. The wreckage of the plane was discovered the following summer, but none of the 32 marine recruits that perished in that crash was recovered.

In 1981, 11 of 22 climbers scaling the mountainside were swept away by an avalanche caused by an ice wall that broke away and were seemingly consumed by the mountain. Mountaineers continue to tackle the challenging slopes, but history has made it clear that Mount Rainier can be a dangerous and fickle place.

One More Eerie Thought

After Callaghan and Stevens went missing in 1909, a park ranger of the day used a formula that suggested the glacier moved at a rate of 10 inches a day. With that in mind, the bodies of the missing mountain climbers from 1909 could reappear around 2011.

The Little Guy
Who said bigger was better? The small city of Spokane, with a population of almost 200,000, packs a lot of power. But it's perhaps best known for being the smallest city to host a World's Fair, an honor it earned in 1974.

Ferry Traffic

Puget Sound is a beautiful place with 14 prominent islands and many smaller ones. At low tide, there can be as many as 786 islands—and if you live on any of them, you'll need competent transportation to get to the mainland. As a result, Puget Sound boasts the largest ferry fleet in the U.S.

Don't Go There

If you were a member of the U.S. military, a trip to Aberdeen was a no-no until the early 1980s. That's because liberal gambling, violence, prostitution and drug use gave the community a reputation for being the roughest town west of the Mississippi in the early 1900s.

Creative Talent

If you love playing the games Pictionary, Pickle-ball or Cranium, you might be interested to know that all three games were invented in Washington.

Beatlemania

I don't know how you can actually confirm this bit of trivia, but legend has it that Seattle was the first city in the U.S. to play a Beatles song on the radio.

Historic Name

Bean's Bight, located on the south shore of the city of Bainbridge Island, was first named Restoration Point in 1792 by Captain George Vancouver. He chose the name to honor British King Charles II, who had been restored to the throne.

A Package Deal

Folks at the Seattle Space Needle have devised an interesting souvenir product with a particular audience in mind—those of us who haven't managed a meal at their infamous revolving restaurant. With the slogan "If you can't eat at the needle, eat the needle," packages of Space Noodles, made from 100 percent, certified organic, semolina flour, are sold in 12-ounce bags. The noodles are Space Needle replicas measuring about one inch in height. If you're interested, a bag of Space Noodles will cost you $5.99.

ABOUT THE ILLUSTRATOR

Roger Garcia

Roger Garcia immigrated to Canada from El Salvador at age of seven. Because of the language barrier, he had to find a way to communicate with other kids. That's when he discovered the art of tracing. It wasn't long before he mastered this highly skilled technique, and by age 14, he was drawing weekly cartoons for the *Edmonton Examiner*. He taught himself to paint and sculpt, and then in high school and college, Roger skipped class to hide in the art room all day in order to further explore his talent. Currently, Roger's work can be seen in a local weekly newspaper and in places around Edmonton, Alberta.

ABOUT THE AUTHORS

Gina Spadoni

Gina grew up in Shoreline, Washington. The Pike Place Market, full of people, foods, and art, was her favorite childhood spot. Her other favorite place was the library, where she spent many happy hours curled up in a sunny window seat. Her love of words led her first to a BA in Journalism from Seattle University and then an MS in Library and Information Science from Simmons College. She began her career in the busy high-tech sector in a job with a major software company. These days, she makes her home in Seattle. Gina recently left the corporate world to focus on writing and art.

Lisa Wojna

Lisa Wojna, author of two other non-fiction books, has worked in the community newspaper industry as a writer and journalist and has travelled all over Canada, from the windy prairies of Manitoba to northern British Columbia, and even to the wilds of Africa. Although writing and photography have been a central part of her life for as long as she can remember, it's the people behind every story that are her motivation and give her the most fulfillment.